TRAVELLER EDUCATION
accounts of good practice

TRAVELLER EDUCATION
accounts of good practice

edited by Chris Tyler

Trentham Books
Stoke on Trent, UK and Sterling, USA

Trentham Books Limited
Westview House   22883 Quicksilver Drive
734 London Road   Sterling
Oakhill   VA 20166-2012
Stoke on Trent   USA
Staffordshire
England ST4 5NP

First published 2005

British Library Cataloguing-in-Publication Data
A catalogue record for this book is available from the British Library

ISBN-13: 978-1-85856-308-4
ISBN-10: 1-85856-308-9

Cover photograph: *Outside Essendon C of E Primary School, Hertfordshire. Photo by Kate Stockdale (Herfordshire Traveller Education Project)*
Back cover: *Ann Marie Egan outside Hertswood Secondary School, Hertfordshire. Photo by Anne Jefford (Herfordshire Traveller Education Project)*
Our thanks to West Midlands Consortium Education Service for Travelling Children and the Derby and Derbyshire Traveller Education Service for the photographs in Chapter 12.

Designed and typeset by Trentham Print Design Ltd., Chester and printed in Great Britain by Cromwell Press Ltd., Wiltshire.

Contents

Foreword

Chris Tyler

Many people working in education are waking up to the fact that the underachieving minority group in (or often not in) our schools are Traveller children. As long ago as 1985 the Swann Report came up with its then remarkable conclusion that the key barrier for Traveller children was actually getting into school (DES 1985). The Office for Standards in Education (Ofsted) have consistently concurred, 'Gypsy Traveller pupils are the group most at risk in the education system' (Ofsted 1999). Rightly, this academic history enabled us to chart the broad perimeters of this bleak situation. Yet probably as a result, when considering the educational needs of Traveller children, there is a tendency to opt towards a deficit model of ability, experience and worth. True, there is no doubting the degree of challenge that Traveller children, their parents and educationalists face when aiming to achieve a quality education. But the focus has until now tended to be upon the *what*. What Traveller children are doing or not doing in our schools. Little has sharpened our ability to address the *how* – how to address this worrying situation.

Somewhat belatedly, central government is beginning to offer a lead through its Aiming High agenda, which aims to advise schools on raising the achievement of minority ethnic pupils. The publication of *Aiming High: Raising the Achievement of Gypsy Traveller Pupils* (DfES 2003) has given schools some general pointers regarding good practice. It is therefore timely to draw together more extensive explorations and accounts of good educational practice that practitioners have found really do work with Traveller children.

About this book

Two concepts underpin this book. The first is a recognition of the need to examine and make concrete the pedagogy of Traveller Education. Inherent here is the recognition of this strand of educational theory and practice, in its own right. The phrase *Traveller Education* is still new. To examine its methods is still to chart new waters. Secondly, a recognition of the collegiate nature of Traveller Education. Forged at the margins of ethnic minority education, much of the work to raise the achievement of Traveller pupils has been achieved through the sharing of practice between Traveller Education Services (TESs) – sharing training, advice and resourcing. This book celebrates this work. Contributors come from across the country, from the urban and the rural, from those at the chalk face and those at policy level. For this is the strength of Traveller Education.

Such is the height of the mountain of Traveller pupil underachievement, we must assail it first at structural level. Accordingly, the early chapters explore the educational policy and whole school responses to Traveller children within the current context. A context which, with its focus upon inclusive education, offers positive prospects for those working in the field of Traveller Education. But there is still remarkably little quantitative research into the statistical nature of Traveller pupil underachievement or non-attendance. For the reader interested in this aspect, Foster and Horton offer statistical insight from across seven London boroughs.

There follows an exploration of innovations in access to Early Years provision for Traveller children. The lack of possibilities for Early Learning can stymie a Traveller youngster's education even before statutory age, so we are interested in access to Early Years provision and this remains a key focus. Claire Norris describes one TES's changing responses to the challenges of mainstream access. Anne Jefford and Kate Stockdale give clear guidance on integration and learning for highly mobile Traveller children, once access has been achieved.

Giant steps have certainly been made in terms of Traveller children's access to primary education. Chapters by Lorna Daymond and Margaret Wood describe access to resources and across schools in Key Stages 1 and 2 respectively.

However, the challenge is most acute at the secondary school phase. Again, as Ofsted have concluded, 'Although some (Traveller pupils) make a reasonable promising start in the primary school, by the time they reach secondary level their generally low attainment is a matter of *serious concern*' (my emphasis) (Ofsted, 1999). Their concern affirms the long road that still needs to be travelled to enable Traveller children to reach their full educational potential. We explore secondary attainment both at macro, policy level, offering insights into innovations such as a Self Review framework, and at micro, individual school and pupil level.

An historical and legislative note

This book need not rehearse the historical and legislative facts that underlie previous research, save to note that Travellers include within their number our oldest minority ethnic group, the Gypsies, and that legislative and cultural records prove that Gypsies arrived in this country in the sixteenth century; a fact that has still to be recognised and embraced in the curriculum. At this stage however, it suffices to remember the depth of history that centres on these minority groups.

Similarly, only a few legislative facts are relevant here. Firstly, both Gypsies and Irish Travellers are identified and recognised by law as minority ethnic groups and as such the Race Relations Act 1976 and its subsequent additions and amendments pertain to them. Secondly, when they are not travelling (and travelling is best defined to include attendance at culturally related events as well as for work related activities), Traveller children should attend school, full time, until reaching statutory school leaving age and LEAs have the duty to educate them. Any other legislative pointers, such as the Education Act 1944, that aimed to protect Traveller parents from unfair prosecution by recommending a minimum level of attendance, need to be seen in this light.

A note on terminology

We refer throughout to Travellers. This is a commonly accepted term that embraces members from a variety of groups, all of whom share a current or recent commonality in that they are members of nomadic groups. The main groups encompassed within the term are:

- English Gypsies
- Irish/Scottish/Welsh Travellers
- Fairground and Show people

- Circus people

- Romany Gypsy refugees and asylum seekers

- New Travellers

- Bargee and water craft Travellers

- Others, such as migratory seasonal workers

Using 'Traveller' about members of any of the above groups is a useful and safe shorthand and avoids some of the culturally loaded meanings that have dogged travelling communities for centuries. The child in the classroom might be a member of a family who is proud to call themselves Gypsies, with all the inherent history this term implies, whereas another family might reject the label because their roots and traditions stem from a different branch of nomadism. The term *Traveller* encompasses all but, if in doubt, teachers should ask the children or their parents. To show an informed and genuine interest to a family about who they are could be a fruitful avenue towards an inclusive, diverse curriculum.

The term Gypsy is often used as a derogatory term in schools. When it is used in a verbally abusive way schools' staff need put in train the agreed methods for challenging such behaviour. It shows sensitivity and knowledge to give the word Traveller a capital T. If we are using Traveller to encompass Gypsy, which stems from Egyptian, both Gypsy and Traveller should be capitalised.

There is no one, real Traveller group, only different branches of a widely spreading nomadic tree with differing levels of mobility, differing educational needs, hailing from different cultural roots. Travelling patterns for certain communities can be predetermined, most notably the Easter to Bonfire Night travelling season of fairground Travellers. This has stimulated the educational response (increasingly using Information Communication Technology) of Distance Learning, pedagogy explored here by Ken Marks. But in most cases travel can be unpredictable, erratic or even rare.

Within the Traveller groups levels of nomadism or mobility vary considerably. The Traveller children in the classroom might be from a highly mobile 'roadside' group whose length of stay in the area might be short. Or they might hail from a housed Traveller family, who despite their accommodation status, might have a proud cultural traditional. Jim Donovan's work in inner London, which he describes here, is specifically about this group, about which little has been written. His work also references Romany refugees and asylum seekers. The demise of the Soviet bloc brought in increasing numbers of these Travellers. Many of the issues and methods described in this book relate to this group. However they have other educational needs and responses, most notably English as a second or additional language and stress related issues stemming from trauma, and these require more specific educational responses.

This latter group also reminds us that the situation regarding Traveller groups is not constant. As one group settles, so another brings new requirements. So there can never be one correct approach to the education of Traveller children. None of the contributors here claim to have got it right for all Travellers. None will claim to have all the answers. What this book aims to do is to pose the correct questions and then begin to examine some of the answers. It is up to practitioners themselves, at whatever level, to explore their own good practice and for us together to begin to right the educational wrongs levelled for generations against Traveller families.

1

Inclusive school – exclusive society: the principles of inclusion

Arthur Ivatts OBE

What is inclusion? And what of its opposite, exclusion? Any journey along the inclusion road must begin with a clear road map of what inclusion means for Traveller children. This chapter sets out the principles of inclusion, reminding us of why and how Traveller pupils are systematically excluded from the education system.

Introduction and aim

In terms of the history of education, the 1990s may well be seen as the decade of inclusive education. Perhaps a major catalyst to the firm establishment of this seemingly new educational construct was the UNESCO Salamanca Statement made in 1994. This concerned itself primarily with the importance of including, as far as possible, children with special educational needs, into mainstream educational settings. Over the following dozen or so years, the notion has been taken much further and now permeates educational policy and practice at almost every level. The prescription for inclusion, while initially recommending actual physical inclusion, now pervades many aspects of education. These include equality of access to all opportunities for girls as well as boys, inclusion of cultural diversity in curriculum content and learning opportunities, inclusion through teaching style and pupil organisation. The inclusion of all children into similar mainstream, happy and successful learning situations, irrespective of differences in class, ethnicity, culture, language, religion, sexual orientation or personality type.

Thus the notion of inclusion has perhaps been helpful in bringing clarity and a unifying perspective to the reality of equal opportunities in education. The international concept of inclusive education now encompasses the enrolment and successful participation of all groups of children in mainstream education and a corresponding change in teaching, curriculum, organisational structures, resources and cultural understandings.

What is inclusion?

This chapter explores why so many schools, with the informed support of Traveller Education Services (TESs), almost uniformly experience frustratingly slow progress in securing satisfactory inclusion, access to education and equal standards of attainment for many Traveller children. To understand why, we need to look at a much bigger picture and ask several fundamental questions.

The term inclusion has become a useful and good sounding word within the context of legitimate professional sound bites. Although apparently simple and straightforward, the concept has a number of problems including indiscriminate use with, at the same time, a hidden diversity of meaning and interpretation. Professional language and even jargon is organic in character. New concepts and practice need a distinctive language to describe and promote them – inevitably spawning shorthand words and acronyms. But there is always a danger that the new language, particularly in its early days, can have a confused status and a vague meaning. It is within the collective interests of educationalists, therefore, to allocate time and try to give clarity to the notion of inclusion, and to identify its implications for policy and practice in relation to Traveller Education. This is, after all, step one of any good practice model.

During the nineteen nineties, the notion of social inclusion developed at political level and contributed to the fortification and promotion of inclusion in the realm of educational policy and practice. Inclusion was part of the New Labour government's philosophy and firmly on the agenda of public administration. Its importance was given added poignancy by the establishment of the Social Inclusion Unit attached to the Cabinet Office at the very heart of government. However, the broadening of the notion of inclusion in relation to special education needs (SEN) to the much wider concept of social inclusion imposes a more complex set of issues. For example, the motivations for the previous exclusion of pupils with SEN was more rooted in the process of people wanting to treat children equally, unless they differed in a way relevant for special provision, than a process of social exclusion based on prejudice and discrimination. It is clearly much easier to agree on changes in what is seen as a relevant educational difference, than to root out deeply held social and racial prejudices.

The semantics of professional terminology, however, may not seem to be directly relevant to the development of educational policies aimed at including Traveller children into happy and successful educational experiences. Educational inclusion is now so well established that all schools are inclusive, and are legally required to be so. The teaching profession now recognises inclusion as a central part of its concepts and aims repertoire and generally understands that a truly inclusive school and classroom will be friendly and right for all children irrespective of whether they are Travellers, or from any other background.

Legislation clearly lays out the inclusion requirements in terms of duties, protections, rights and entitlements. Admission regulations and race relations law ensure equality of access to school places. The Office for Standards in Education (Ofsted) makes specific reference within its inspection advice to both schools and inspectors, that an evaluation will be made of the quality of a school's policy on inclusion. International prescriptions and constraints fortify national assurances. In addition to the Salamanca Statement, there are the European Union's (EU) Directives on antiracism, xenophobia and non-discrimination in education. The EU 1989 Resolution on School Provision for Gypsy and Traveller Children is still relevant. International Human Rights legislation and the United Nations Convention on the Rights of the Child stand now as firm markers for all societies in terms of how they should view and treat children. Inclusion is a common theme identifiable either explicitly or implicitly within this veritable arsenal of children's rights.

Over the years, schools up and down the country have been aided by the tenacious efforts of TESs who have provided the advice and vision of what educational inclusion looks like for Traveller communities. For many schools this has required a reassessment of both practice and attitudes, but generally schools have been professionally responsive. Traveller children in these circumstances have experienced happy and successful learning with a growing sense of personal confidence in both learning and identity, born of the school's high expectations and affirmation of their cultural and ethnic background.

It might seem that the policies aimed at educational inclusion for Traveller children had been successfully achieved but the evidence, including recent reports by Ofsted, reveals continued restricted access, poor attendance, disaffection and marked underachievement. The situation demands further, detailed research.

The principles of inclusion

Certain questions should be asked in relation to policies aimed at inclusion. What does it mean to be included? Is it a sense of well being or a warm feeling of being part of the whole? What is the essence of the whole social world that one is to be included in? Is it essentially a notion of conformity, politically motivated to secure social control? Or, more cynically, just about not being seen as riven by unemployment, crime and disaffection? How do we measure successful inclusion in education: through attendance, behaviour, or achievement?

Finding answers requires honest and informed analysis of the causes of the social and educational exclusion of Traveller communities in the first place. This might usefully be understood as the first of seven principles of inclusion.

1. Why exclusion?

The first principle of inclusion is to understand why exclusion exists for these particular minority ethnic groups. There are a number of factors:

■ Widespread racial prejudice and discrimination at individual, community and institutional level

■ These groups occupy a despised social status, and in sociological terms, fulfil a scapegoat function for the majority society

■ A long-standing fear and bureaucratic hatred for nomadic communities has resulted in a history of racist abuse structured within legislation over four centuries

■ The development within these communities of a culture which is resilient, independent and sharply focused on survival in a hostile social and political environment

■ Poverty and material deprivation are major contributors to actual and/or perceived social exclusion

- A nomadic lifestyle which restricts opportunities for social integration and inclusion in a society that is almost exclusively structured and organised for a sedentary population

- The lack of will and understanding in education at all levels to appreciate the link between inclusion and levels of achievement

- The lack of understanding by schools of the difference between formal, on paper inclusion (which can mask an invisible culture of exclusion) as opposed to genuine acceptance of pupils irrespective of their background. This might be called the ghost of inclusion

- A false view of human intellectual capacity and the consequential impoverished level of professional thinking and use of professional language that represents an abuse of children's intellectual integrity. For example, references in some school inspection reports to the less able and the most able

2. The changes needed

Given such significant hindrances to inclusion, any attempt at securing effective and successful inclusion would include an audit of the changes required to remove or short circuit the structural and cultural forces of exclusion. Particular points are clear to see.

- The minority ethnic status of Traveller communities needs to be more widely publicised, understood and accepted. More affirmative statements are needed from government and the Commission for Racial Equality (CRE). The Social Inclusion Unit would have to readjust its priorities and be explicitly inclusive of Traveller communities

- The government and the CRE need to make a direct contribution to setting standards in public life and administration, which are appropriate to Traveller minority ethnic status. They should, for example, instruct government that the terms Gypsy and Traveller always have a capital initial letter and the CRE could indicate this style to the press, to publishers of English dictionaries and other media. Such instructions and initiatives should be given suitable publicity, including press conferences

■ All race equality training by government (including the armed forces) and local authorities, should specifically include Travellers

■ The right to a nomadic lifestyle must be facilitated and clearly enshrined in law and local authorities should have a duty to make adequate site provision and respond without prejudice to planning applications for private residential site developments

■ Amendments to, or repeal of, all laws which discriminate against Traveller communities and other nomadic communities. The Traveller Law Reform Bill should be passed and other necessary legislative actions taken

■ Representative, consultative and focus forums should be established to facilitate the development of policies, provision and practice that is informed and influenced by the needs and wishes of the Traveller communities themselves

■ For there to be equality of treatment under the law, particularly in the application of the legislation concerned with race relations and public order, the media need to change their tune. Ways must be found to dissuade the media from publishing material that is an incitement to racial hatred and which would not be tolerated for any other minority group in the United Kingdom

■ The Crown should issue a formal apology to the Traveller communities in Britain for the Acts of genocide against Gypsies in the sixteenth century and for the subsequent racial persecution and social exclusion

■ The languages, history and cultures of the Traveller communities should be recognised, respected and celebrated in the national cultural consciousness, for example by establishing a national folk museum devoted to nomadic communities in Britain, past and present

3. Negotiating inclusion

The process of inclusion cannot be rushed and must depend on negotiated inclusion, in that both the group to be included, and the including society, can agree a set of terms and conditions for inclusion without any coercion by the includers. The terms might include:

■ That institutional structures, such as schools and colleges, act fairly without prejudice and discrimination and become places where access and equal treatment are assured

■ Inclusion should not be secured under duress but only with the willing consent of the Traveller communities

■ Avoiding any terms and conditions set by the majority which amount to saying 'If you behave in the way we want you to, then you will be included'

4. Inclusion best understood

The fourth principle is that the terms and conditions need to be judged for their relevance and fairness against our best understandings and interpretations of national and international law in regard to Human Rights, race equality and equal opportunities. Cultural assimilation would not, therefore, be seen as a legitimate condition. Including a group within schools, without the corresponding response in terms of teaching, pupil organisation, the curriculum and cultural understandings, will be ineffective and is incompatible with models of educational inclusion that are soundly based.

5. Respecting optional exclusion?

Social inclusion also requires an understanding and respect for those who for whatever reason, do not want to be included. Such individuals and groups can act as a thermometer for the health or malaise of a society at large and should promote on the part of that society a process of reflection and self-evaluation and on-going analysis of its dominant value systems. Society should be structured so that its margins are organically inclusive and socially procreative. For example, New Traveller communities could be viewed as exploring alternative lifestyles that might be part of the solution to the impending global catastrophe. Consequently, communications need to be established with isolated and/or non-participatory communities in a positive context, to ensure that there is a sharing of ideas, safety for the vulnerable and access to services when required.

6. Inclusion across the whole

Strategies aimed at social inclusion need to be consistent and comprehensive. Policies for social inclusion need to reflect co-ordination at both local and national level and for the two spheres of actions to be compatible. For example, it is counter-productive to try to be inclusive at local level when national policies facilitate or even promote social exclusion, as in existing policies concerned with site provision and evictions. Policies need to be comprehensive and wide ranging and thus require inter-agency structures at local and national levels. To place successfully in school a Traveller child who is feeling happy and secure and ready to learn, requires actions by a range of departments and agencies working within a consistent policy context. For example, it is little use having a welcoming school up the road if the official site and its location reflects public neglect and social exclusion; if the facilities make it particularly hard for young parents to get their children ready for school and when the transport department claims that the 1.9 mile journey along a busy country road with no lighting or footpaths is safe. It is also important that policies for social inclusion should be cross generational. A policy to include children will fail if the parents or the youth of the community are left out of policy considerations.

7. Inclusion for all
My final point is that the motivation and process of social inclusion should not automatically focus on people and groups at the lower end of the socio-economic spectrum. It may be that some religious groups or those with excessive wealth feel excluded by their ambivalent status and atypical lifestyle.

Understanding inclusion/exclusion – whose job is it?
Monitoring and evaluating the models of good practice developed by schools and Traveller Education Services should not be too self-critical. The wider picture needs to be kept in mind. Those responsible for the promotion of policies for inclusion, together with those vested with the duty to inspect its effectiveness, should bring to their respective work a more realistic analysis of the causes of exclusion and the structural changes required to eliminate it. This will help give the professionals and institutions implementing policy a fair chance of success. This is in their interests and, more importantly, in the interest of the groups to be included. The complexity of this model of inclusion must be recognised.

It has often been said that if the education for Traveller children is right, then it will be right for all children. The serious concerns and questions raised by Traveller Education Services over the last few years are now promoting at local education authority level a more critically informed assessment and analysis of policies aimed at inclusion. This is not to detract from the significant success so far. But the daily routines of implementing policies on inclusion increasingly illustrate for the practitioner the need for the issues identified within the bigger picture to be part of inclusion policy at a strategic level. The *Aiming High* (DfES 2003) policy initiative by the Department for Education and Skills represents an awareness of the big picture issues and is to be welcomed.

2

Traveller Education and the Strategies

Brian Foster and Hilary Horton

Based on Traveller children's achievement data gleaned from seven London LEAs, the authors analyse the effects of the National Primary Strategies. They surmise what pedagogical responses are possible and identify the implications for all parties involved in raising the achievement of Traveller children.

Introduction

Most Traveller parents would identify the acquisition of basic skills as the main purpose of their children's education, and Traveller Education Services (TESs) tend to focus on literacy and numeracy in the support they give to children in school. When Labour came to power in 1997, it identified joined-up solutions as a key theme, requiring centrally funded initiatives to reinforce rather than undermine or duplicate each other. As a result, Traveller pupils have been mentioned as a target group of many initiatives and Ofsted have clear guidance to inquire about the inclusion (Ofsted, 2002a) and progress of Travellers in mainstream schools (Ofsted/Audit commission inspection guidance, 2002). The National Literacy and Numeracy Strategies now amalgamated as the National Primary Strategy, radically changed the teaching and learning of basic skills in primary schools and consequently required the role of teachers and teaching assistants employed by TESs to be modified.

This chapter considers the impact of the Strategies on the achievement of Travellers across seven London local education authorities (LEAs) which have been monitoring achievement for some years. We analyse these to identify ways in which class teachers, senior management teams, TESs and LEAs can work together to ensure that the strategies are effective in helping close the gap between the achievement of Traveller pupils and their peers.

The achievement of Travellers

Seven LEAs[1] in London belong to a consortium, which facilitates the sharing of good practice and monitoring of Traveller education. The consortium has been collecting data on attainment of Traveller pupils since 1996 and trends in attainment over a period of years can be identified. At any time, there are approximately 800 Traveller pupils in consortium schools, although turnover rates[2] range between 40 per cent and 75 per cent each year. Charts 1 and 2 below show the proportions of pupils achieving at or above expected levels at KS2 since the Strategies have been operating. The achievement of Traveller pupils in the consortium is compared to the average achievement of all pupils in the consortium, LEAs and the national averages.

These graphs suggest that:

■ Traveller attainment is significantly below national and LEA averages

■ Traveller attainment in English is lower than Maths

■ The gap between the attainment of Travellers and other pupils is not closing in Maths and is widening in English

These conclusions must be set in context. A high proportion of the Traveller pupils tested had disrupted educational experiences, which may have contributed to their underachievement. For such pupils, level 3 at KS2 may be a positive achievement, but the 'at or above expected level measure' fails to recognise this.

Educational continuity and progress

A more reliable measure is the progress made by each pupil between consecutive Key Stage tests. Levels of mobility are such that less than half of the pupils tested at KS1 were tested in the same authority at KS2.

1 Camden, Hackney, Tower Hamlets, Greenwich, Southwark, Lambeth, Waltham Forest

2 (No. of arrivals + number of departures)/Number of school age Travellers in LEA during academic year) cf. Dobson J. and Henthorne K. (1999) *Pupil Mobility in Schools* DfEE Research Brief No. 168

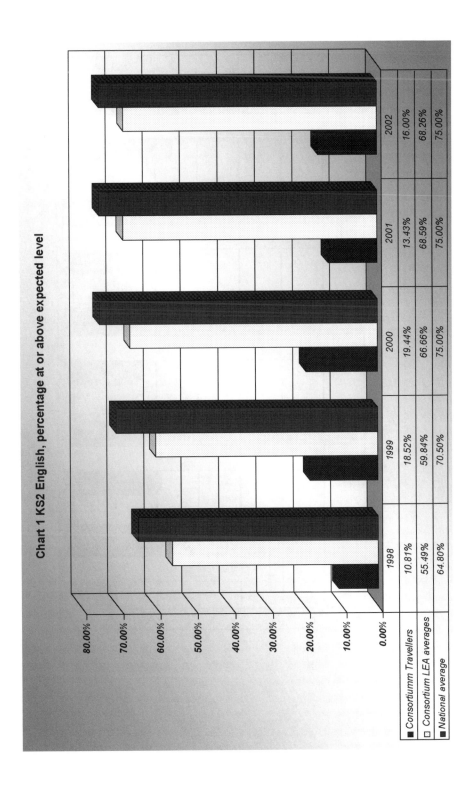

Chart 1 KS2 English, percentage at or above expected level

	1998	1999	2000	2001	2002
■ Consortiumm Travellers	10.81%	18.52%	19.44%	13.43%	16.00%
□ Consortium LEA averages	55.49%	59.84%	66.66%	68.59%	68.26%
■ National average	64.80%	70.50%	75.00%	75.00%	75.00%

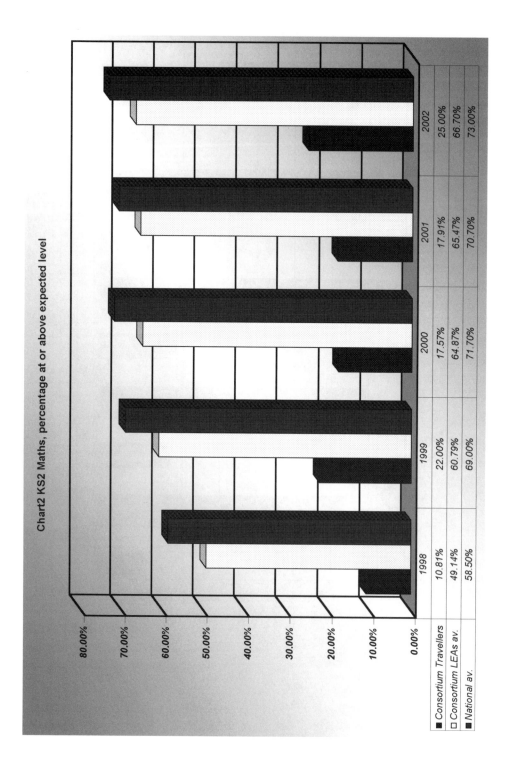

Chart2 KS2 Maths, percentage at or above expected level

	1998	1999	2000	2001	2002
■ Consortium Travellers	10.81%	22.00%	17.57%	17.91%	25.00%
□ Consortium LEAs av.	49.14%	60.79%	64.87%	65.47%	66.70%
■ National av.	58.50%	69.00%	71.70%	70.70%	73.00%

Progress KS1 – KS2 (average = 2 curriculum levels or 12 points)		English			Maths		
		below av. (<12 points)	average (12 points)	above av. (>12 points)	below av. (<12 points)	average (12 points)	above av. (>12 points)
Girls	14	2	5	7	4	8	2
Gypsy	2	-	-	2	1	1	-
Irish Traveller	9	1	4	4	2	6	1
Roma	3	1	1	1	1	1	1
Boys	8	3	5	-	3	2	3
Gypsy	3	-	3	-	-	2	1
Irish Traveller	4	3	1	-	3	-	1
Roma	1	-	1	-	-	-	1

Table 1

Of 50 (excluding absent or disapplied) Traveller pupils who were tested at KS2 in 2002, only 22 had been in the same LEA for KS1 tests. Nevertheless, the progress of this small group of children provides an indication of what is possible where Traveller children have a stable educational experience. Table 1 shows that over 70 per cent of Traveller pupils made progress at or above the expected level between KS1 and 2.

Half the Traveller girls, but none of the boys, made above average progress in English. In Maths the pattern is reversed with three out of eight boys making above average progress, but no girls doing so. The data reveals worrying trends for the boys. Not only are most boys failing to close the gap with their peers, but the sample size is smaller, due we believe, to the fact that Traveller boys in years 5 and 6 are more likely to be excluded, to exclude themselves or to be exempted through disapplication on grounds of Special Educational Needs.

Parallel experiences – the achievement of other minority ethnic groups

As the Strategies were implemented it became clear that the impact on certain groups was less than had been hoped. The strategy for primary schools, Excellence and Enjoyment 2003, acknowledges ethnic minority underachievement:

> Though many children from minority ethnic backgrounds are already achieving at the highest level there is still a great deal to do. On the whole children from black Caribbean, black African, Pakistani and white working class backgrounds are still performing less well than from other groups, and worryingly the performance of black Caribbean pupils appears to get worse compared with that of other pupils as they go through primary school. (DfES, 2003a p42)

Travellers are not included in this summary because ethnic monitoring of Travellers only began in January 2003 when the additional categories of Gypsy/Roma and Traveller of Irish Heritage were added to Pupil Level Annual School Census (PLASC). However, the Ofsted study of four ethnic minority groups in seventy schools, *Raising the Achievement of Minority Ethnic Pupils* (Ofsted, 1999) found 'Gypsy Traveller pupils are the group most at risk in the education system.'

In 2002 HMI found that the gap in performance between boys and girls (at KS2) had remained at 9 per cent since 1998. Girls are now 16 per centage points ahead of boys in writing at the end of KS2. This is exactly the same gap as in 1998 at the outset of the Strategy (Ofsted, 2002b).

Although the headline figure of percentage achieving expected level has risen, the 'long tail of underachievement', in which many Traveller pupils find themselves, has not shortened: 'the percentage of pupils below level 3 has not decreased in recent years despite (the Strategies) support' (DfES, 2003a p41). The HMI review of the NLS at the end of the third year concluded:

> While the Framework has been welcomed by many schools, they often express concerns about the pace of teaching for pupils with SEN which they consider too fast and the lack of time to revise work or to provide more intensive teaching (Ofsted, 2001a).

The failure of the Strategies to reduce Traveller pupils' underachievement can therefore be seen as part of a broader picture.

The Strategy response to underachievement

In order to address these and other deficiencies the DfES has developed a model of intervention for children experiencing difficulties in literacy or mathematics, based on three waves:

> Wave One. The effective inclusion of all pupils in a high quality, daily literacy hour and mathematics lesson (Quality First Teaching).

> Wave Two. Small group, low-cost intervention for example, booster classes, springboard programmes, or other programmes linked to the National Strategies, like Early Literacy Support (ELS).

> Wave Three. Specific targeted intervention for pupils identified as requiring Special Educational Needs support (DfES, 2003a p41).

Berger and Gross (1999) argued that the Literacy Strategy could contribute to inclusive education. It sought to raise teachers' expectations of pupils and supported them by setting clearer objectives. The predictability of the literacy hour, with daily short periods of teaching followed by opportunities for exploring and practising what they have already been taught, could benefit children with limited attention spans and literacy skills. The sharing of texts, which pupils might not be able to tackle on their own, enabled them to hear and use language more complex and subtle than they could read independently. Children could contribute orally, and teachers, by skilful questioning, could direct children to aspects appropriate to their level. This is the basis of

Quality First teaching which should meet the needs of 85 per cent of pupils.

Wave 2 initiatives are short-term interventions, usually involving teaching assistants working with small groups of children to put them on track to achieve expected levels in Key Stage tests. Government guidance is that 10 per cent of children should receive Wave 2 support. The content of the intervention and training programmes has been developed centrally and LEAs provide training for teachers and teaching assistants.

Traveller children outside the Strategies

Additional funding and training is provided for Wave 2 initiatives but they are a scarce resource to be targeted on those children likely to derive the maximum benefit from them. In our experience, Traveller children are seldom given the opportunity to benefit from these initiatives. In some cases, such as Additional Literacy Support that targets pupils achieving level 1 or 2C at KS1, Traveller pupils may not have the phonological awareness to participate fully. In the Consortium LEAs between 30 per cent and 50 per cent of Travellers achieve below level 1 at KS1. If pupils arrive mid term or have an erratic attendance pattern, many schools will not be willing or able to include them in Wave 2 initiatives.

The precise nature of Wave 3 interventions has not been specified by the DfES but there is an expectation that they should be carefully selected so that the pupils can make at least double the expected level of progress over the intervention period. They will be funded from the additional needs element of formula funding to schools. LEAs and schools are expected to identify appropriate strategies and map out what is available, who should benefit and what the entrance requirements should be.

Some interventions that could be offered in Wave 3 have been shown to make a significant difference to Traveller pupils. Traveller pupils who received Reading Recovery support achieved level 2B or above at KS1 and continued to achieve at or above expected levels through their school careers. Reading Recovery uses a trained teacher in a one-to-one setting with a Y1 pupil, for 30 minutes each day over a period of several months. The rate of catch-up is significant and the intervention has a positive impact on learning across the curriculum, and on self-esteem and confidence. But its cost and the narrow age range it targets have restricted its use.

Other schemes, such as 15 Minutes-a-Day, are less intensive and expensive initiatives developed from the principles used in Reading Recovery and these can achieve the expectations of Wave 3 initiatives. Talking Partners uses oracy to develop speaking and listening skills and model writing strategies.

Traveller children and special educational needs (SEN)

Wave 3 overlaps the new SEN Code of Practice (DfES, 2001). The working definition of SEN has been extended to include children who are achieving at more than one level below their expected National Curriculum level, even if they do not have learning or behaviour difficulties. This presents something of a challenge to Traveller Education because we have long argued that lack of or disrupted education does not constitute a learning difficulty. The new Code of Practice relies more on action supported by the school and class teacher, and less on external help, so the SEN label may not carry the stigma it once did. In reality it is inevitable that Travellers will be drawn into the SEN fold if they are going to benefit from Wave 3 interventions.

In our view, Wave 3 should be the point at which the strategies pick up those Travellers who have fallen through the nets of Waves 1 and 2. But our experience also suggests that schools and TESs need to be vigilant to ensure that Travellers do not discover holes in this final safety net. The DfES intends that only 5 per cent of pupils should fall into the Wave 3 category. Our data shows between a third and a half of Travellers achieving at more than one level below age appropriate expectations. Travellers often attend school in deprived areas where levels of achievement are well below national averages, so there is a concern that pupils requiring such support will not receive it. Wave 3 includes some of the most expensive provision and, when it falls within the Code of Practice, requires parental consent and co-operation. There can be cultural implications for some communities. For example, most Eastern European countries have consigned Roma children to Special schools as a form of educational apartheid and Roma parents are understandably wary of any system which involves labelling their children.

Implications for practitioners

TES co-ordinators need to have effective working links with the Strategy teams in their authorities. They should monitor the impact of the strategies on Travellers across the LEA and share the results of their analyses within their authority.

With the inclusion of Traveller groups within the PLASC categories we anticipate growing concerns within LEAs about their levels of achievement. TESs will have an important educative role in making their authorities aware both of the limitations of the PLASC categories, and the importance of devising strategies for tackling underachievement at an authority level. Inspection and Advisory services need to make enquiries about the progress of Travellers in the schools they support (Ofsted, 2001b, p42).

TES staff need to keep up to date with developments within the Strategies, be aware of the LEA interventions available (in provision maps) and the ways in which Travellers can benefit from them. This is no small task.

Strategy co-ordinators, SENCOs, Ethnic Minority Achievement (EMA) co-ordinators and senior management teams within schools need to ensure that systems for monitoring the impact of the Strategies include Travellers, even though they may be a numerically small group. Schools need to understand that the Travellers have reasons to conceal their ethnicity, so they should not rely on the PLASC categories alone for internal ethnic monitoring of achievement. TESs should determine with schools those children whose families have identified themselves as Travellers.

Schools need to be sensitive to social and cultural issues that interfere with the ability of Traveller children to benefit from these interventions. We would argue that levels of Traveller underachievement are so serious that positive action is required to address the issue. Traveller pupils should be given the opportunity to participate in appropriate interventions, if they are educationally capable of benefiting from them, but in addition the school and TES should take steps to address the social and cultural issues that might limit the benefit they derive. High expectations and ownership of learning objectives by pupils will have a positive effect upon educational outcomes.

HMI have advised, in our view correctly, that schools should deal directly with Traveller families (Ofsted, 2001b p42). This should be the objective of all interventions by the TES, ultimately leaving families as independent and confident users of the education service. The TES will then have a monitoring and mediating role, as relationships develop. In some cases, TES staff may need to act *in loco parentis* to ensure children receive their entitlement to support.

Class teachers and Strategy co-ordinators need to make sure Quality First Teaching includes children from diverse cultural backgrounds, whether or not there is an associated language issue. HMI commented: 'Schools with pupils from Traveller communities provide some good examples of focused support and commitment to partnership in teaching ... Curricular targets are being included into action plans for supporting pupils from Traveller communities' (Ofsted, 2001a p29). TESs produce material which can be used in Strategy hours and there is a module for Year 5 term 2 based on the big book, *The Travelling People* (see Wormington, 2000; Delamere and Warton, 2002).

Monitoring progress needs to inform practice through use of data from P scales (DfES, 2001a), optional SATs and formative assessment (see Black and William, 1998) to identify appropriate interventions and their effectiveness, at Wave 2 and Wave 3. The expectation is that Wave 3 initiatives should achieve double the expected rate of progress over the period of the intervention and systems are needed for monitoring this. TES staff should have a clear and distinct role in the process recognised in the school's provision map.

Conclusion

On the evidence presented above, using the Government's preferred measure, the Strategies have not yet had a significant impact on the achievement of Travellers and similar groups. However, Traveller pupils who have stable educational experiences are beginning to make reasonable progress between Key Stages. The Strategies continue to evolve and develop to address the needs of underachieving groups and there is evidence (DfES, 2003a) of some movement towards styles of teaching and learning which may be more inclusive for Traveller pupils. Our experience in Traveller Education suggests that there is always a danger that Travellers, for reasons beyond their control, will miss out on or benefit less from initiatives designed to meet their needs. Close monitoring is needed at all levels to evaluate access and impact of every intervention. There has to be close collaboration between schools, families, TESs and LEAs to secure the basic skills entitlement for all children.

3

Meeting the needs of Traveller pupils – principles and practice

Chris Tyler

Starting with broad principles then moving on to pedagogy guidelines, this chapter outlines good policy practice for schools in their educational responses to Traveller children.

A number of principles underpin best practice approaches to enhance the educational experiences of Traveller children in our schools. This chapter concentrates on key pointers that schools can use to develop staff pedagogy that will improve the educational achievement of Traveller children.

Though it might sound like stating the obvious, it is vital that the school knows the background of all its children. The enrolment of a Traveller child can raise questions about its curriculum organisation and delivery. Senior managers in school need to take cognisance of the general and specific nature of the Traveller communities they serve and ensure that this information and any relevant guidance are relayed to all staff. This is more effective when there is a clear demarcation of role responsibility in the school that culminates with a specific senior member of staff. There is an assumption that any good school knows its community, yet one still finds reticence to reach out and include the school's local Traveller community. Designating a member of staff for outreach work can be the important first step.

A Traveller child's path to school will seldom be straightforward. Transport provision might be involved, demanding communication and organisation agreements with third party service providers and parents, uniform might need to be provided, investigations made about their previous educational experience and support sought from other educational agencies such as a Traveller Education Service (TES). All these elements of access require co-ordination and information transfer, as well as outreach work to the family. So a first principle is to establish who will liaise with other agencies, hold and seek background information, and relay as appropriate. Designating one person, known to all, will help.

Starting points and target setting

Organisation of support and relay of information is often agreed through the expertise of a special educational needs co-ordinator (Senco) or pastoral head of support. With their link to a senior member of staff as described above, the individual class or subject teacher has the back up to find an educational starting point.

The school needs to assess the child's educational ability before they can determine an appropriate curriculum. This, allied to target setting, must be sensitive and accurate, especially when enrolment takes place outside of the normal starting date. An educational baseline has to be established, especially in literacy and numeracy.

Once the child's ability is known, targets must be set. This common practice is vitally important for Traveller children. Short-term targets allow the children to see progress in the immediate context. Facilitate an educational basis for discussion with parents. Enable links across subject staff, in secondary schools and between Senco and classteacher in primary schools and lay the foundations for future continuity of the children's education from the outset.

Apply the principles underlying SMART target setting: Specific, Measurable, Achievable, Realistic and Time Related. But that is only the start. Targets have to be small enough to enable progress but significant enough to be meaningful. They need to be appropriate to the individual and so can encompass a variety of curriculum and non-curriculum (such as behaviour) areas. The Traveller child will benefit from SMARTER BUT targets, meaning:

- Specific (have clear performance related aims)
- Measurable (precise, not vague)

■ Achievable (small steps starting at the correct point)

■ Realistic (not too many, enough to be achieved)

■ Time related (to allow consolidation)

■ **Evaluated**

■ **Reviewed**

and, in addition:

■ **Built into the existing curriculum structure**

■ **Understood by all staff**

■ **Targets that have a shared ownership by class/subject teacher, child, parent**

These principles help ensure that the teacher teaches each Traveller child to the optimum while building in mechanisms to maximise educational input within the constraints of planned or enforced mobility and striving for educational continuity.

The school as inclusive mirror

Research confirms that all children perform better in an environment that recognises and welcomes them.

> Where the presence of travelling children is openly acknowledged, and where accurate and positive images of the different nomadic communities are featured within both the resources of the school and the curriculum, then the response is lively and there is a genuine openness to learning. (Ofsted, 1996)

So principles of inclusivity must be actively pursued and promoted at all levels of the school and must be all encompassing. Every staff member, from Head to ancillary, has a part to play in this active development and enactment of curriculum and resources and the implementation of paper policies and ethos. The inclusive work that is initiated in the classroom must also be built on outside the classroom.

Travellers will travel

To embrace Traveller communities means that the school must come to terms with the reality that at some point in their educational life most Traveller children and their families will travel. To recognise that mobility is practically inevitable means that the school can prepare itself to minimise unauthorised absence, maximise home/school relations and build a continuous inclusive curriculum.

From principles to practice – starting on the right note

To achieve a quality education for Traveller children requires schools' staff to be flexible. Prior to enrolment and access to school, senior secondary schools' staff needs to determine an appropriate timetable and how it will be realised. If a Traveller pupil is entering secondary school outside of usual admission times, a senior manager should develop a clear plan for admission, integration and induction. The plan should incorporate the roles of outside agencies such as the Education Welfare Officer (EWO) or the local TES. Most schools admit pupils other than Travellers outside normal admission dates, so it is useful to have in place pre-planned arrangements.

At secondary level, attendance part time might be appropriate at first for children who have been out of school for a long time. But this should be treated with caution as it means the child is being excluded from their right to access full time education. The option is only suitable when it is decided in consultation with parents that an agreed phasing in will lead up to eventual full time attendance. Alternatively, the new pupil might initially access only parts of the curriculum. The underlying aim is to achieve early independence for pupils, so their confidence in coping with the right subjects at the right level has to be built. Part time attendance is rarely appropriate at the primary level. Both primary and secondary schools are strongly advised to place children in their correct year groups.

Ethos and policy are discussed below but it is worth noting here that welcoming begins at the school's front-line staff and reception area.

First steps and monitoring progress

All teachers and schools have numerous ways to start off newcomers on a welcoming, friendly footing. Only once the children are settled can initial educational assessment be carried out so appropriate targets can be set. Be aware of any possible cultural bias in the assessment tools. In this stressful moment in their educational career, the children need to be enabled to perform at their peak in assessment tasks, so that the results are accurate. Many schools use short-term target setting recording pro forma. These allow accurate recording of academic progress and give the classteacher or Senco the opportunity to enable consistency of input across a range of mainstream and support staff.

The school might use a simplified version of its target setting records specifically to assist liaison with parents. Again, this need not apply only to Traveller families. Giving details of academic targets, successes and next steps facilitates informed debate with all parents.

Such measures feed into the vital element in SMARTER BUT target setting: consistent, regular review which ensures that achievement is monitored systematically. For Traveller children this is vital, as gaps in learning may disguise their achievement. It is important for teachers who have the overview of the children's educational development to monitor closely how and where they are achieving and feed appropriate next steps back to other staff.

Finally, Traveller children should be involved in setting and monitoring their own targets. Uncertainty or disjointed educational experience makes it especially important for the children to receive feedback and, importantly, praise.

Now that feet are under the table

Once Traveller children are established in their class, needs related issues may arise. At primary school, lack of early learning experience might result in their needing more time to explore their new environment and experiment with play equipment. They may have had few formal play opportunities and possibly require some familiarisation with board games or construction toys.

The teacher can advocate the importance of early learning experiences for the younger siblings of the pupils they teach. Discussions with parents on the role and activities of the nursery, plus an escorted taster visit will help to promote this vital opportunity for the younger children. Liaison across the school might generate the development of loaned Early Learning Boxes or Book Bags which offer a selection of early learning activities (see chapter 7).

Teachers should encourage co-operative play and learning opportunities. This will be of particular importance if the Traveller children have not had access to the opportunities for socialising with their peers outside of the school setting and requires support in unstructured periods of the school day. Similarly, playground or lunchtime supervisors might need specific training in how to integrate Traveller children through co-operative play.

The behaviour of Traveller children is often cited by teachers as a cause for concern. The school needs to broach behavioural issues in a systematic and responsive way. The children might not be aware of the expectations or norms expected of them. Forthright verbal responses to adults including teachers might not be a symptom of 'bad' behaviour but rather a reflection of the accepted language codes used at home. As with many issues relating to Traveller children, it is vital for staff to take a step back from the representation of behaviour and see it within its context. They will then be ready to react by explaining expectations rather than immediately enforcing sanctions. Rules and codes must certainly be ultimately enforced but these must be explained to parents and children before they are enforced. Handled sensitively, the school will find willing allies in the parents for such enforcement.

Achieving inclusivity

Senior teachers and governors have a particular responsibility to ensure that an ethos of whole school inclusivity pervades and underlines the curriculum. Inclusivity is characterised by communication of accurate and pertinent information, willingness to involve and engage with marginalised sections of society and the promotion of active efforts to include all the school's community in all its activities.

To achieve all this will require the school to go the extra mile. Relations with parents are paramount. Early links with parents should be only the beginning of an on-going process. Communication with the parents should centre on the positive, not wait until a moment of crisis. Support agencies such as the TES or an EWO will be helpful. Special arrangements might need to be made at first to encourage Traveller parents to attend parents' evenings and events. Any reticence might be more to do with having insufficient information than with disinterest. Lack of information may be due to their low literacy levels or unfamiliarity with the education system because of their own inexperience.

For these reasons, all communication to the child's home needs to be sensitive. It is important to know the literacy levels of the parents but enquiring about it should not appear to be prying into their pasts. Many families with low literacy levels have a support network to deal with written messages from school but an inclusive school will also arrange to pass on information verbally.

In the early stages, a home visit, possibly supported by the TES or EWO can be useful (see Home/school liaison below) but this depends on the family having some knowledge of the school.

In the optimal situation, an inclusive school and curriculum will so involve Traveller parents that they look to the school to act as advocate over non-educational issues. I am not promoting the school as an advice service, but such relationships are an expression of the trust formed between school and home, proving that going the extra mile has worked. Interestingly, this notion of the school as a one stop shop for a variety of services underlies recent Government thinking for the future of combined education, social and health services.

Resources and challenging racism

In line with all public bodies, the Race Relations (Amendment) Act 2000 requires schools to actively promote race relations and equal opportunities and to eliminate discrimination. Outside of the cities there may be few ethnic minority pupils at a school. In these mostly white environments, teaching and representing the breadth, history and richness of the Traveller cultures is one sure way schools can play an active part in meeting their legal requirements.

Included in the Act is the responsibility upon schools to develop a policy to deal with racial harassment. Following the Stephen Lawrence Inquiry Report (Macpherson, 1999) the Home Office accepted the definition of a racist incident as 'any incident which is perceived to be racist *by the victim* or any other person' (my emphasis) (Home Office, 2000). It is vital that schools are unequivocal about racist behaviour such as name-calling directed at Traveller children. Staff should be clear about what is and is not racist. The school's policy should state clearly what a member of staff should do in response to racist incidents. Senior management should stress to all staff that this applies to incidents involving Traveller children. Traveller pupils can be the victims of racism but find themselves being punished when the causes of conflict have not been properly investigated. At the induction meeting, the school can explain to parents and children its policy and responses to racist behaviour. Parents will thus be apprised of the school's intent and their creation of a safe learning environment for their children.

Home/school liaison

If there is a solid bridge between home and school, some Traveller parents will quickly liaise on the school premises with the appropriate staff member. Others will need encouragement and facilitation, while still others will not be receptive. It is the job of schools to assess where parents are along this continuum and take appropriate action.

All communication with Traveller parents should be assessed for its clarity and whether the most effective form of communication is being used (see 'Achieving inclusivity' above). Informal school based discussions should be set up as soon as possible, possibly starting with a home visit. The object is to enable Traveller parents to avail themselves of the equal access to staff afforded to all parents, usually on the premises. Health and safety procedures need to be in place prior to such visits.

At its fullest, liaison with Traveller parents can be enriching for all concerned, especially the children. Input from parents to school assemblies or class based curriculum work is a strong bridge builder. School based adult literacy classes or after school hours activities can powerfully affect the entire family by advancing skills and developing parents' abilities to support their children. Parents engaging in adult learning also give a clear signal to the children that the family as whole values education. The pedagogy of family learning can be extremely beneficial to Traveller families.

Whole school planning

Many of the methods described here are complex and will best be achieved by developing whole school responses that incorporate these practices. Worked into or appended to the school's overall plan of development, this gives the opportunity to address practices systematically so as to cover:

- identified pupils or year groups
- stated objectives
- proposed strategies to be employed, including resources to use in training
- key success criteria
- monitoring processes
- named lead responsibilities

Such approaches are common in many schools but are particularly valuable when supporting Traveller families (see example of a whole school plan in appendix 1).

A whole school approach has the advantage of gearing the whole staff towards agreed targets and has them working within agreed structures to enhance the overall curriculum. It provides the structure for senior staff to motivate the achievement of the Traveller children as a group and measure it against that of the majority school population. It incorporates into whole school target setting issues such as numbers of Traveller parents attending school consultation events. The overall aim is to put into practice polices and strategies that are targeted specifically but met collectively.

What happens if they go?

The effective education of Traveller children must include rehearsal and acceptance of the scenario of their moving. Effective, coherent and trusting on-going home/school liaison is essential, so that families have the confidence to announce their travelling patterns well in advance. Having this information allows the school to contact the receiving school or TES and to co-ordinate their collation of the pupils' records. It is vital to pass on full information to future schools so as to enable continuity of the pupils' education.

In some circumstances, most notably with fairground families, Distance Learning programmes should be prepared. These bridge gaps between school attendances but must be effectively managed and organised (see chapter 13). Schools may also wish to promote school attendance through promoting parents' own abilities to access education, for example by issuing client held TES contact information (available from a local TES or the DfES). Moves towards client held educational records are still in their infancy, but the groundbreaking RED book (DfES/National Association of Teachers of Travellers, 2002) is available from TESs and represents a step change in encouraging the consolidation of learnt targets and identification of next steps.

To protect the continuity of Traveller children's education, the pupil registration regulations were amended some years ago to allow for dual registration of Traveller children.

> The school that they normally attend when not travelling will be regarded as their base school. They can register at other schools tem-

porarily while away from their base school. Base schools must keep a place open for Traveller pupils who are travelling, and record their absence as authorised while away travelling. (DfEE, 1997).

Conclusion

The issues that Traveller children and their families raise can be challenging for schools. But Traveller children in the classroom can bring with them experience from beyond the immediate locale of their classmates. Their knowledge of a different world and different values, often values that we in the sedentary community have lost to our detriment, can enhance the whole school community. There is no doubting the commitment of the vast majority of Traveller families to education for their children, a commitment honed from centuries of denial of access.

The road towards meeting Traveller children's educational needs is still long. But the provision of a welcoming ethos and an affirming curriculum will begin to meet those needs, while allowing us to enrich our schools to the ultimate benefit of all children.

4

Policy into practice

Lucy Beckett

Drawing heavily on the supportive role of TESs, Lucy Beckett considers what a good policy basis would be for schools striving to be proactive in its support for Traveller pupils. She describes how to convert policy into all-important practical strategies and reminds us of the problems (and solutions) that underpin all this work, specifically around data collection.

To examine Traveller Education at policy level requires detailed analysis of education management and administration. Policy originates at central government level before linking with local government processes of decision making and administration – a top down model of policy making. The emergence of grant funding for Traveller Education and the changes which have taken place, currently in the form of Standards Fund grant, are the result of a government department aiming to bring all funding initiatives in line with government policy. However, channels of communication can be used, such as links with the DfES, to have inputs into a bottom up policy model. This brings examples and evidence of good practice in Traveller Education to the attention of government departments, local authorities and schools, elected members and Ofsted.

Key players in stimulating this communication are the Traveller Education Services. TESs have government support and approval through the DfES, HMI and Ofsted for their work that has created a national network and has enabled continuity by putting policy into practice, within a framework of human rights, race equality and equal opportunities.

The role of the TESs

The policy work of TESs follows government guidelines and a legal framework on social inclusion and multi-agency working. A characteristic of Traveller Education work is a focus on both macro and micro levels of policy and practice. These levels range from the classroom with the child and family, to the whole school, to the TES team itself, to the local education authority and also to national and international levels. For example, *Aiming High: Raising The Achievement of Gypsy Traveller Pupils* (DfES, 2000), was the result of a synergy between the Department and TESs.

Partnership is important for effective responses to mobility. Joint planning and review, achieved through partnership, characterises good practice. Working in partnership with a school, a TES supports Traveller children to gain access to education so that the school can include them in mainstream education. This support includes the effective use of support programmes, distance learning and other resources. It is therefore important that advice and support is sought from the TESs. Outreach support, for example on working fairs, is often available. This increases the individual support to pupils, enabling them to do practical science and maths tasks even when away from their base school. Support is also given to pre-school children in developing early learning skills.

Other examples of effective partnership working are:
- joint work to develop policies, such as behaviour policy
- joint work to create school development plans
- in-service training
- discussion with teachers concerning pupil files, pupils' work, individual education plans and reports
- celebration of culture
- working with parents
- liaison with a range of agencies to encourage the registration and attendance of travelling children
- support to secure the entitlement of children with special education needs

An Ofsted inspection would focus on how a school ensures effective continuity of learning, for example how it assesses, keeps records and how expeditiously it works to secure the entitlement of its Traveller children with special education needs. TESs offer training in these areas.

They have an important role in evaluating equality practices in relation to Travellers. In so doing, possible inequalities may be highlighted and underlying causes can be addressed.

As it moves from policy into practice a school can continue to use its TES because it is important to evaluate both. Effective communication between school and TES will enable this to happen. Examples of communication are:

■ a TES teacher meeting weekly with a school link person to update and plan

■ a TES teacher attending Connexions meetings in school

■ regular discussions with individual school staff to ensure that pupils maintain progress

■ regular review meetings

Schools should try to make full use of all of forms of support the TES can offer and thereby create an effective partnership.

Equality for Traveller children in the operation of a school's policies and practices can be assessed by close examination of those policies and practices.

School management

The local education authority (LEA) can monitor the education of Traveller pupils on roll through the TES. Good school management is characterised by:

■ serious commitment to meeting the educational needs of all pupils including Traveller pupils, recognised within an equal opportunities policy and the school development plan

■ the recognition that the educational responsibility for the pupils rests not with the TES but with the school and the classroom teacher

■ taking seriously the need to involve parents in partnership and having a realistic notion of what this involves

■ TES support being used in partnership in shared policy and practice

- ■ implementing administrative structures which try to achieve educational continuity, for example by promoting record card procedures or providing distance learning packs

- ■ the acquisition of appropriate resources and information to facilitate curriculum developments which would include positive images of the Traveller communities

Schools' provision for spiritual, moral, social and cultural education that takes into consideration Traveller pupils can only be addressed adequately by working in partnership with the TES. As part of its curriculum provision, schools should also be active in seeking advice.

As education institutions are bound by legal duties, such as the Race Relations (Amendment) Act 2000, they must assess the impact of all their policies on ethnic minority pupils, staff and parents. Equality targets should be framed as outcomes for Travellers and based on adequate representation, parity of treatment, fair and equal access procedures and how organisational procedures and decisions affect them.

Pupil admissions

The information needed is:

- ■ the number of Traveller pupils on roll over the course of the academic year

- ■ any evidence of active steps taken to ensure that admissions processes are fair and equitable to Traveller pupils

- ■ an account of the process for admitting Traveller pupils to school.

Assessments

Evidence is required on whether a school compiles ethnic data on pupil achievement and progress, test and exam results. Also the allocation pattern of pupils to groups/sets/streams and reports analysing pupil attainment and progress. Assessment methods should be checked for cultural bias and action taken to remove any identified bias.

Raising attainment levels

Evidence is needed to show that assessment outcomes are used to identify the specific needs of Traveller students and inform policy, planning and the allocation of resources. It is important to monitor whether teaching methods encourage positive attitudes to ethnic and cultural diversity.

Delivering the curriculum

Evidence should show how curriculum planning takes account of ethnicity, background and language needs of Travellers, and how teaching methods and styles address those needs.

Discipline

These questions can be asked:

- do schools compile ethnic data on discipline issues and behaviour?
- does the school have a behaviour policy?
- are the school's procedures for discipline and behaviour management fairly and equally applied?
- is there reporting on and evaluation of any discrepancies, for example, a disproportionate number of Travellers being disciplined?
- are Traveller parents fully involved in the discipline/sanctions process if necessary?
- do staff receive in-service training on discipline and behaviour management?

Pastoral guidance and support

TESs need to know if Traveller students are being offered the guidance and support they need to make full use of school. Staff should be given training and resources to guide and support Traveller pupils effectively. Data should be compiled with reference to strategies for guiding and supporting Traveller students. And a crucial issue: how is information about pupil achievement passed to Traveller parents?

The impact of an equality policy

TESs analyse how a whole school approach has been adapted to promote equality for Travellers, how staff and governors are involved and kept informed about the policy.

Exclusion

There should be data on the exclusion rates for Travellers and specific targets in school action plans to reduce the number of exclusions.

Addressing racism and racial harassment

Every school's race equality policy should have an action plan and this should clearly set out the procedures for dealing with racist incidents and complaints. All staff, including support and ancillary staff, should be trained to deal effectively with racist incidents. Traveller students should be specifically indicated as a group in the policy .

Curriculum teaching and learning

School action plans should have targets for improving the attainment of Traveller pupils. TESs, who have a focus on Traveller pupil achievement, should support this. There should be strategies in place for tackling any disparities in the attainment and progress of Travellers compared with non-Traveller pupils.

Membership of a governing body

- schools should actively seek governor representation from the Traveller community

- there should be a governor with responsibility for Traveller matters

- data should relate to formal contacts between the school and parents

- the school should ensure that governor support is appropriate for Traveller pupils

- there should be evidence showing details of training programmes for governors, including data on attendance and on nominations for attendance at training

Parents and communities

Policies should outline strategies for school contact with and involvement of Traveller parents. There should be data relating to contact with parents, consultations with parents and role models used.

Proactive steps should be taken to involve Traveller parents with school and encourage people from the Traveller communities to become school governors. Reports should evidence evaluations of consultations and strategies for involving Traveller community groups.

Support, advice and guidance
Evidence should show that a whole school approach is used to promote equality and eliminate racial discrimination. Also, that diversity is recognised as a positive feature of the school. All staff should be trained to deal with incidents of racism, racial harassment, prejudice and stereotyping and taught that this affects Travellers.

A sensitive and structured system of support should be available for Traveller students and active links should be established with the TESs to enable this.

Comparative analysis
Questions here can include, what are the issues affecting Traveller pupil achievement? Also, are they the same or different for other groups of children?

Analysis should look at the outcomes of assessments and the impact of policies on pupils, staff and parents, as well as the impact on Traveller students.

Moving from policy into practice – mobility needs
Mobility is a fact which TESs are expert in dealing with in relation to education. Mobility creates needs. Such as:

- swift admission to school
- better access to the whole curriculum through careful planning
- improved equality of opportunity in inclusion strategies, including admission to schools
- access to SEN services
- access to early years provision
- access to 13+ provision-to 19
- improvement in academic achievement

- development and improvement in home school links

- improved levels of attendance across all phases

- development of learning programmes for 14+ Traveller students to ensure access to education to 16 and up to 19

- improved continuity of education for all Traveller children.

Equality in action – practical strategies for schools

Any policy is meaningless unless it is translated into practice. Schools can use specific strategies to meet needs such as those identified above. These include providing effective links between home and school, focusing on attendance. Also, ensuring there is a clear policy for meeting Traveller needs in school, plus its assessment, monitoring and review to ensure Traveller children's entitlement to the curriculum.

Identification of Traveller pupils needs

A needs analysis could be compiled of a number of different factors including:

- accommodation status

- attendance – the pupil may need support prior to school placement or through a school induction programme

- a route needs to be established back into school following an absence

Behavioural and social factors

Support may be required in establishing appropriate patterns of behaviour in the classroom, in learning the behaviour codes appropriate to the playground, in developing relationships with peers and in acquiring the social skills needed for self management.

Emotional support

Support may be needed:

- because there is perceived victimisation, or the child is the subject of racial abuse

- in starting a new school, due to frequent changes in school

- to raise self esteem in school

- because of family circumstances particular to the Traveller communities, such as weddings or horse fairs

- because of problems with living circumstances such as eviction or loss of home

Learning

Support may be needed:

- in the acquisition of literacy skills

- because of the lack of school experience / early learning skills

- in acquiring skills and participating in the curriculum because of absence due to cultural factors

- in completing homework/coursework

- Special Education Needs

Health

The family may need support in regard to health issues that relate to the children's learning situation.

Parental liaison

The family may need information on the organisation of schools and the process of learning.

School issues

The school needs support and information to ensure that the curriculum offered to the children reflect their own life and family background and to understand the behaviour patterns of the children and the social conventions of the Traveller family.

The TES and school need to work together to access statutory support for the child.

The TES and the LEA need to work together in contacting or communicating with families and other departments and there is a need to liaise with other agencies concerning pupils' needs and education.

Specific observations and assessments

These may focus on experience of school and would include school records and also on the children's development and self-esteem or levels of disruption and their relation with peers. Liaison with parents also needs to be evaluated. Pupils' language, including literacy/reading age/asking appropriate questions/following instructions, and their national curriculum levels all need to be assessed.

Independent activity

An analysis may be needed on the pupil's confidence in class or contributions to group activities. Also, their motor skills or how much use is made of equipment/ICT and what proportion of teachers' time is taken up with the Traveller pupil.

The need for differentiated work

TES support can be utilised with reading materials, worksheets, time to complete work, extra instruction, overall objectives for pupils. Specific support strategies will maintain the quality of provision.

Problems and challenges – a matter of data

Even where policy is in place to underpin and inform effective practice, such are the needs of Traveller pupils that there are still bound to be challenges for the school. There are complex issues around data collection, mobility and Traveller students. However, the Pupil Level Annual School Census (PLASC) alone is inadequate to address these issues. Ethnic monitoring complexity is a major contributory factor in PLASC and many individuals are left out.

TESs collect a great deal of information and data over the course of an academic year. They take into account factors that PLASC does not, such as:

- dealing with students from communities that are mobile
- collecting data in retrospect (of necessity)
- that a snapshot count is grossly inaccurate
- that there is no account of students who do not fit ethnic categories
- that there is no account of those whose parents choose not to fit categories

■ that PLASC does not take account of a needs based analysis

   ■ nor under 5s

   ■ nor of those not on roll

   ■ nor of education at home

   ■ nor of high mobility

   ■ nor of fairground and circus children

   ■ nor of unknown future admissions

Solutions

TESs' data is therefore a far more reliable way of gaining information on Traveller education issues and this should be acknowledged by schools, LEAs and policy makers at government level. There needs to be a more sophisticated system of monitoring and of data collection and analysis. Data and information must take account of long-term outcomes, identification of needs, the honesty of data, Best Value and tracking. There should be information and clear definitions about underachievement, disadvantage and discrimination.

At a national level, strategies need to be developed and linked to the local level for collecting adequate data that is verifiable. A thorough analysis of the issues that prevent appropriate and meaningful analysis is needed. How best to support successful strategies for the collection, validation and use of data needs to be given consideration and the importance of TES work should be acknowledged. It is without doubt TESs who have the best information, data and expertise on the enhancement of access and achievement of Traveller students.

Conclusion

Specialist TESs enhance the capacity of schools and indeed LEAs to address the needs of the most disadvantaged minority communities in British society. TESs provide clear, coherent thinking and policy on the meaning of underachievement and achievement in relation to school development and planning. They have professional expertise in relation to socially excluded groups and have understanding and knowledge about good practice in the area of Traveller children's achievement. TESs also work with an extensive range of other departments and agencies.

TESs deal with complex and multi-dimensional work, including mobility issues, ethnicity issues and discrimination issues as part of the framework of their work. Those who work in Traveller Education are best placed to address the questions around the issues for Traveller Education.

5

Tackling access and attendance for Traveller pupils in Leeds

Claire Norris, Carol Ward and Sue Itzinger

Leeds Traveller Education Service has thirty years experience in support-ing Traveller children in schools. Norris, Ward and Itzinger describe their adaptable, changing patterns of support.

Introduction

Travellers' Education Service (TES) in Leeds was established in 1975 when one teacher was appointed to support children attending a primary school near the new council Traveller site in Cottingley. It soon became evident that there were a large number of other children from both the site and roadside camps who were not accessing education. The TES's number of teachers grew and initially delivered education by taking a school bus, adapted as a mobile class-room, round the sites and roadside camps. Though not ideal, this developed good relationships between Traveller communities and the TES, enabling children to be successfully accessed to Leeds schools. Thanks to commitment from Leeds City Council and now Education Leeds, we now have a strong and successful team of fifteen.

Transport and the roadside team

Close to each other are two permanent council Traveller sites in Leeds, three miles away from the nearest school. There are also several private sites and a fluctuating number of roadside camps.

In 1985, we decided that the main obstacle to these children accessing school was the task of getting them physically to and from school. Many parents had only one vehicle, which was used for work. We therefore had to establish a routine of daily attendance at school using transport.

TES transport from the sites and camps to schools has proved to be a key factor in the children's continuity of school access. It allows children to attend the same school no matter how much they move around the city. This has been particularly successful on the council site where we now have children successfully attending secondary school.

But transport was not the only barrier, as we still had children who were not accessing school. This was for a variety of reasons such as high mobility and slow admissions procedures. Taking steps to address these issues resulted in the establishment of a specialist roadside team. The team of two teachers worked three days a week doing outreach work with roadside families, working closely with targeted schools and the Pupils Admissions Service. This enabled the TES to give quality time to meet with new families, locate the children who wanted school, assess their needs and to find them appropriate placements quickly. Educational work was given to the children on the school bus while they awaited a school place. This worked well for the children who needed little or no support in school, but not when there were larger numbers and they needed support.

Roadside team + induction team = access

In order to overcome these barriers we formed an induction team. This team of two teachers was to be responsible for school placement and induction.

The roadside team inform the induction team of any children who need school places, providing names, dates of birth, school preferences, locality, school experiences and whether they have a RED book (DfES/ National Association of Teachers of Travellers, 2002) or not. Using their knowledge of school places and liaison with the Pupil Admissions Service, they can identify a school place, usually with a choice of schools, within two days. An accompanied school visit for the children and parents is promptly set up. Other arrangements are also made, such as the completion of admissions forms, uniform, free school meals – if needed – and school policies are explained.

After this visit an Induction Contract is made with the school. This states the time and dates of TES support – a week for a primary school, two weeks for secondary – the support being until 10.30 each morning.

If the pupil needs extra support beyond this time, the school is re-quested to complete a TES Referral Form. If the school has not had Travellers recently, in-service training (inset) is offered. In addition, a member of staff visits in the first two weeks to introduce the latest high quality culturally appropriate resources, and the school is encouraged to buy through the TES. Our up-to-date *Cultural Resources Catalogue* and information leaflet is left with the school to assist them to buy further resources.

If transport is required, it is arranged and both school and families are given details. The Induction Team then meets the children on their first day at school, along with appropriate member of the school's staff.

An initial assessment is made of each child. This is either done in their home or on the first day at school, depending on times and suitability. The assessment is to determine their literacy and numeracy levels. A copy is kept with the TES in order to monitor progress. The school is then able to set appropriate work.

During the induction period the Team support the school to integrate the children fully into the classroom and the school's routine. This is achieved by: establishing buddy systems, supporting the classteacher, providing equipment, liaising with the family, supporting the children and dealing with any problems.

Thanks to a dedicated Induction Team staff, since setting up this system in 2003, 100 per cent of those children requesting school places have been accessed successfully.

Support for access – the transition times

Transition can apply to moving from home to nursery, nursery to primary, primary to secondary and secondary to further education or work. These can be difficult times for families and children.

The TES is split into two teams: Nursery/Primary School and High School, the latter concentrating on improving secondary education for Traveller pupils. It was apparent that there was a problem with the pro-cedures used to allocate high school places, due in part to parents' failure to return school preference forms. To address this problem and monitor all transition, a member of the High School Team was allocated the role of Transition Co-ordinator. This has led to a 100 per cent of Year 6 Traveller pupils being successfully allocated a secondary school place.

The transition support includes visits to parents to complete and send school preference and pupils admissions forms. The contact with the families continues until the child is successfully integrated into secondary school. Support with appeals is also available to parents. Staff is allocated to targeted pupils and families to support their attendance at secondary school open days and new parents evenings. The families are also shown the DfES video *Are you missing out?* (DfES, 1998). Transport to school is arranged when needed. Help and advice are given on school uniform, school meals and similar issues.

Target families are contacted towards the end of August to make sure everything is in place for a successful start to their new school.

In September, targeted children are supported into their new schools and schools are checked to see if the new pupils have arrived. Any children who have not started are followed up and the schools informed of any relevant information.

Support for access – post 16 transition
The Key Stage 4 Co-ordinator monitors the transition at post 16, working closely with the Careers and Connexions services. In January of each year, every pupil in this age bracket attending school is checked to ensure that they have a career programme in place. Those pupils who are not attending school are offered support in the form of advice on college courses and suitable employment, help with applications and supported visits to college open days,

Tracking attendance and tackling non-attendance
The TES collects annual attendance from the moment Traveller children start school. However, we need to be alert to any attendance problems before a child has spent too much time out of school. As the number of Traveller children in schools increased, it became clear that we had to monitor attendance closely and that this would require a different system. We now have a dedicated team of three who have responsibility for attendance in nursery, primary and secondary schools.

Each Monday, faxes are sent to schools who have had Travellers on roll, requesting them to return the information for that week in register form. This is recorded and a designated member of staff follows up children with two or more unauthorised absences by phoning the school and family and, where necessary, visiting to ensure a swift return to school by dealing with any problems raised. Any action taken is recorded. This is supported by school based education welfare officers (EWOs) and the school attendance officers who ensure that Traveller pupils' families are telephoned on their first day of absence. Monitoring is underpinned by regular liaison between the TES and senior members of the Education Welfare Service (EWS). Pupils causing concern are discussed and joint action involving school based EWOs taken when needed.

At these meetings it emerged that some schools were marking pupil absence as 'B' for 'Based off site'. This is normally used to indicate that a pupil is being educated out of school, for instance at college or on a school trip. But in most cases the pupil was at home not receiving education. In one case, the school recorded the pupil's annual attendance as 100 per cent by marking the pupil in the register with 'B' for the whole year, when they had not been in school at all. Similarly, the register mark 'T' for 'Travelling' is sometimes used as an authorised absence, when the child is truanting. This problem was brought to the attention of the teachers and also senior managers in the EWS.

With the ever increasing number of schools with Traveller children on roll, currently 54 nurseries and primary schools and 25 secondary and special schools in Leeds, it has become too time consuming to fax each school every week. We therefore target 20 key schools and gain weekly attendance figures from them. Each term we liaise with their attendance officers to discuss ways they can monitor attendance as a key priority, contacting the TES only if there is a particular concern.

Celebrating attendance

At the end of each term, Traveller pupils who have attended 95 per cent or more of the time receive a certificate from the TES. And pupils with the best attendance records are awarded prizes at the end of the school year. In 2001-2002, nine children were presented with attendance prizes. They were visited by members of the TES, who took their photographs and interviewed them for the *Traveller Post Magazine*, a magazine for Travellers nationally, published annually by the TES. The pupils told their interviewers:

'I like school and have lots of friends. I want to work in childcare when I leave.' 14 year old high school girl.

'I love drama and have had main parts in the school productions *Bugsey Malone* and *Grease*. I would like to do acting when I leave school.' 15 year old high school girl.

'I like my school and when I grow up I want to be a nurse or a teacher.' 11 year old primary school girl.

'I like school. When I grow up I want to be a firefighter.' – 6 year old primary school boy.

'I am in year 8 now and I really enjoy school so my attendance is very good. At school my favourite subjects are Drama, English and Maths. My main hobby is dance and I do this at the social club three evenings a week. We put on a show in September and I won a trophy for best achiever. After I finish high school I plan to go to college or university to train as a dance teacher.' – 12 year old high school girl.

And three roadside primary pupils said:

'We like to come to our school, even when we keep shifting. The taxi man is kind and my mam lets him know when we have moved.' 'I like school, I have lots of friends there.' 'I like doing my work at school and I like my teacher.' .

Partnership plus trust equals success

To achieve beneficial and lasting progress it is essential to work in partnership with parents so as to build up good relationships in both the long and short term. Since 1975, the Leeds TES has had few changes in staff so it has established close working partnerships with Traveller communities. There are still problems, though, with families who live in houses, private sites or those who come into the city for a short time and are not known to the TES. And since the introduction of the Traveller ethnicity categories as part of the Pupil Level Annual School Census (PLASC), we are becoming aware of more Traveller pupils in schools. Accordingly, the TES has adapted its services over the past 28 years and will continue to do so, always working in partnership, enhancing trust and helping Traveller children to greater success.

6
Supporting mobile Traveller pupils
Anne Jefford and Kate Stockdale

Integrating new mobile Traveller children into school can be one of the most challenging aspects of inclusion. Two teachers with extensive experience of working in such circumstances examine the roles of the key players involved in ensuring equality of educational access for highly mobile Traveller pupils.

Introduction and aim

After some pre-school experience, most pupils begin school at Reception and gradually learn the customs of the school over many years. Their families too are familiar with the expectations of the education system. But highly mobile Traveller pupils have to assimilate the ethos of each new school they attend very quickly. The challenges that both they and the schools face are acute. To achieve success, every member of staff needs to be involved in the process of integrating these children.

This chapter offers ways to respond to these challenges. It raises the important questions staff may ask and provides answers based on successful school support situations in Hertfordshire. They are not definitive but because they are derived from consultation with schools, they offer examples of good practice.

Headteacher: *How can I ensure pupils are accessed quickly and successfully?*

The preliminary visit

The headteacher of the receiving school is advised to offer the chance for parents and pupils to visit the school before the children start. Staff can then talk to the pupils about their worries, allay parental concerns and answer the family's questions. The headteacher can explain the ethos of the school and take time to explain a few key school rules. For example, families can be assured that name-calling is unacceptable in school, that racism is always taken seriously and dealt with appropriately. Giving the family a tour of the school lets them familiarise themselves with the layout, be introduced to the children's class and meet key members of staff. It is also helpful for families to meet the secretary as this will help facilitate home/school liaison.

Other administrative matters, such as the amount and method of payment of dinner money, can be explained. If there is a school uniform, it is important that children have the correct clothing on their first day so they do not feel conspicuous. PE kit also needs to be acquired before the pupils start. If the school has book bags, then it is essential that the new pupils start with one so they can take a reading book home on the first day.

The headteacher can talk to the parents about their children's previous schooling and use this information to request records from the last school attended. Some pupils carry the RED book (DfES/National Association of Teachers of Travellers, 2002), which details previous schools attended and lists educational targets. If the pupil has one, it allows classteachers to update the pupil's records as well as gaining information on the correct starting point for the child.

The headteacher can inform parents of the activities that take place away from school, for example swimming and educational visits. Traveller parents are sometimes fearful of the children swimming or travelling on coaches and it might be worth offering parents the opportunity to accompany their child. Traveller Education Service (TES) staff may also be able to help with these issues. At this initial meeting, it is advantageous to get permission forms for these activities signed by the parents.

Before this initial meeting ends, the school should ask for contact telephone numbers for the family and also for a taxi company, if one is used. The school telephone number should be given to parents.

Briefing staff

A briefing should be held to inform the whole staff about when the new pupils will be starting and to give them the opportunity to ask about them. Staff need to understand the role of the TES and the nature of the support it offers schools. The TES should discuss the right of every child to education even on a short-term basis and emphasise that the accumulation of positive school experiences, even if for a short while, has dramatic results for Traveller pupils in the long term. This is the time when the TES can be invited to provide in-service training for the school staff. If this cannot be arranged before the pupils start, the head-teacher should consider releasing the classteacher to meet TES support staff during school time in advance of the children's admission.

All staff need to be present at this briefing with the TES, so that issues both in and out of the classroom can be addressed. If midday supervisory assistants (MSAs), learning support assistants (LSAs) and site managers or caretaking staff cannot attend the meeting, time should be set aside to prepare them before the new pupils start.

Keeping the pupils informed

Pupils at the school should be told that Traveller children will be joining the school. If the Travellers are from a highly mobile group, there may be antagonism towards the families. That schools are a haven for children, a safe and welcoming place where every pupil is valued should be emphasised, possibly at an assembly, and the importance of inclusion can be made clear.

One Hertfordshire headteacher has a regular *Welcome to New Pupils* assembly, as her school is close to a transit site and regularly has new Traveller pupils. Such assemblies were originally set up to welcome Traveller pupils but now take place whenever a new pupil joins. This school has made a large book all about the school, to share with new pupils. The book contains photographs of staff, photographs of boys and girls in their winter and summer uniforms, in swimming costumes and PE kit. A few essential rules are listed and a page of photographs showing the diversity of the homes of the pupils: flats, trailers, detached houses and cottages. The new pupils can take home the smaller version of this book and share it with their families.

Flexibility is important

Flexibility is the key to successful access and integration of highly mobile pupils. An LSA should be assigned to assist with settling the children in on their first morning. If they are coming by taxi, it may not arrive until after the school day has started, so this support needs to be put in place in advance.

Playground and lunch time arrangements may have to be adjusted as parents would expect older siblings to supervise the new arrivals and there may be anxieties if they are separated. If their lunch hours or playtimes are at different times, the older children should be allowed to join younger siblings for the first few days until the younger ones have settled. Parents often request that their children be put in the same class even when they are of different ages. This is not ideal, but flexible out of class arrangements can make things smoother for the new pupils in the short term.

It is impossible to predict how long highly mobile pupils will attend the school, but they should be treated like all new arrivals, on the assumption that their stay is long term. Staff should not assume that the children might only be there for a couple of days and should use appropriate, inclusive language that acknowledges that they belong to the school as much as the settled pupils do. Constant reference to *our* pupils and *our* parents, as opposed to the newly arrived Traveller families, does not support an inclusive school ethos.

Classteacher: *How can I ensure pupils are accessed quickly and successfully to the classroom?*

Preparing the class

Prepare the children for the arrival of the new pupils by discussing the steps needed to ensure a welcoming environment. Circle time could be used to talk about it within the context of handling new situations and meeting new people. Appoint a buddy for each new child to help them settle in. Prepare the room, organise a desk for the new pupil, a labelled drawer and labelled coat peg. Ensure exercise books, a reading record and a spelling journal are all ready to give to the new arrival and that their name is on all class lists including those on display in the classroom.

Resources reflecting Traveller lifestyle help to ensure that the pupil finds something in this new environment that relates to their lives. Some appropriate materials should be on display in the classroom, possibly borrowed in advance from the local TES, these can be interesting and useful to the whole class.

If possible, add a Traveller perspective to the week's teaching plans. For example, if the topic is homes, remember to include a trailer in the lesson discussions.

Classteacher: *How can I ensure the pupil has a positive and successful learning experience in my class?*
If you are in receipt of support from an additional teacher or assistant, introduce them to the class and explain they are here to help in the classroom for a while. If a stranger appears in the classroom with no formal introduction, the school is sending out mixed messages about dealing with strangers, and also about inclusiveness.

Assessment and target setting
Pupils with gaps in their learning may doubt their own ability to learn and be afraid lest other children think they are 'stupid'. So they need to be given opportunities in class to show their strengths and the breadth of their experience.

Assessments need to be carried out quickly but sensitively. If pupils feel insecure in the classroom, assessment cannot be meaningful or accurate. Fear of failure may prompt children to say they cannot do anything. Only once they feel safe, can formal assessments and learning begin. TES staff can help with the assessment process. If a child arrives with a RED book, new assessment might be unnecessary. It is important to keep this book up to date by entering all appropriate information where indicated.

The next stage is to set targets. Teachers have to come to terms with the possibility that if a child is only in their class for a short time it may be difficult to see and record progress. But these small targets are built on in each new school and together contribute to the yearly progress of the Traveller child's learning – and knowing this is the teacher's reward. So it is important that teachers and pupils celebrate all achievements. And as many mobile pupils do revisit counties and schools, the extent of their progress can be seen over time. It is essential to keep records of achievement and examples of work to send on to the next school and also to reference on their return.

Classteacher: *How can I place the child to ensure their inclusion?*

When placing the pupil into a class group, be aware that the child's recording skills may not match their academic level. Placing them in a low ability group can be detrimental to their learning. Pupils need to know that you have high but realistic expectations of them and that you will help them realise these expectations.

Traveller pupils need to feel that they belong to the school as much as their peers do, and are of equal worth. Start by adding the child's name to all duty rosters and merit systems immediately so they feel included in the class routines.

Explain the rules of the classroom, for example answering the register, using the toilet, getting out of their seat. These pupils may have attended many schools and rules are different in every school. Children can only abide by rules if they know what they are.

The new pupil may have a different accent, or use words in a different way to the majority of the class and this should be celebrated and not ridiculed. Phrases in common use in school may have a different meaning for the Traveller pupil, for example 'break', 'turn over' or 'look up with reference to books'. Some everyday classroom words or terms may be totally unfamiliar to them, for example house names used for class groups. For some Key Stage 1 pupils, the terms 'literacy' and 'numeracy' may need explaining. Schools, like families, often have their own shorthand or code words that will need explaining to the new-comer.

Do not automatically expect the Traveller child (even the circus or fair-ground child) to be immediately forthcoming about their background. All pupils need to be encouraged to share their culture and the positive aspects of their lives with the class. The presence of relevant resources can help to develop trust.

Give feedback to the parents on their children's first day of attendance as they may have felt worried about leaving their children in an un-familiar setting. Even if the children go home in a taxi, a telephone phone call home to give immediate feedback will be appreciated.

Classteacher: *How might fairground and circus children be supported in other ways?*

Fairground and circus children may attend a school briefly, sometimes only for a week, while they are in the area. These pupils usually carry distance learning packs prepared by their base school (the school that they are enrolled at during the winter period). When they are accessed to school, they will bring their work pack for classteachers to look through the work and to give support with specific problems. Supplementary worksheets could be given but overall responsibility for the work pack – including marking – lies with the constant educational experience, namely the winter school. While the children are in your school, they should generally be integrated into the class routine and follow the week's curriculum.

Circus children are a great source of fascination for the settled community and can find themselves endlessly answering questions about their life. If these pupils are just being used as a human resource their educational needs are not being met. The circus itself might have a link person or informal education liaison contact who is usually happy to arrange for schools to visit the site for an educational visit. The fairground community is served by an official Education Liaison Officer (ELO) who covers their local area. These officers are a splendid source of information and can act as a link for a school that wants to know more about the fairground community. The local TES is the best initial contact to link up with your ELO.

Classteacher: *How can I best utilise Traveller Education Service support staff?*

The arrival of mobile Traveller children sometimes enables the school to access additional support staff from a TES. It is vital that this most valuable resource is used to the full.

This support can be used to assist with assessment arrangements. A support teacher can take the class to give you time to become familiar with target setting or you could observe pupils and then carry out your own assessments. Alternatively, the support teacher can carry out assessment, using TES assessments or school assessments, and inform you of the pupil's level so you can set targets together.

The support teacher or LSA is in the classroom to support you so that you can give the Traveller pupil a successful learning experience. The support can be used flexibly to meet your needs and those of the class, but it is important for you to share your short-term plans with the support staff so you encompass the targets identified for the Traveller pupil. Joint planning can be achieved through a short meeting before school or at break. Together, you can decide how the new pupil will access your plans. It may be necessary to modify them and the support teacher can be asked to differentiate your planned work accordingly. Meetings can be arranged after school for longer term planning, where future topics can be planned to include a Traveller perspective. Most TESs have a wide range of resources to support all curriculum areas and the week's literacy work can occasionally be based upon Traveller specific books.

In-class support can take many forms – whole class team teaching, group teaching and one to one support. Whatever methods are used, make time to share learning outcomes with your support staff to help inform records for future class planning.

Communication between school and home is vital. Support staff can facilitate this for you by taking the class and allowing you to talk with parents. Parents with low literacy skills will have problems with letters that are sent home and could miss out on vital information. They may consequently appear disinterested in what the school is doing. A conversation will help clarify or avoid misunderstandings. Verbal communication with parents ensures that all-important information does reach the home.

There are many ways in which parents can help with learning at home. Some parents may feel threatened by their weak literacy skills and poor understanding of the educational system and appear unwilling to help their children, but if they are given practical strategies they will be encouraged to become involved in their children's schooling.

An example of good practice in Hertfordshire illustrates what can be done. A family Numeracy training course for Traveller parents was set up in four schools. The schools, the TES and the Hertfordshire numeracy team delivered a two-day training programme for Traveller parents in each school. Changes in the teaching of numeracy in recent years were described and parents were given practical strategies to help their children at home. They had an opportunity to observe a numeracy hour in class, to learn the new ways of recording calculations and to discuss their concerns with the school staff. Each family was given a numeracy resource pack with an explanation of how to use it to support their children's learning. In the pack were dominoes, playing cards, dartboards, hundred square, dice, counters, number line, calculator, place value cards and number fans. It also included an illustrated book-let about games using the equipment provided and a video especially made to accompany the resource pack. All this required much planning and effort by the various teams involved but this illustrates the type of liaison that can be achieved when school and support agencies work collaboratively towards a common goal.

Midday supervisory assistant: *How can I ensure playtime is an enjoyable experience for all?*

On the roadside, Traveller children explore their surroundings, digging and climbing, examining everything they find, often in a hazardous environment. They spend much of their time outside, often in charge of younger children. They appear to be less protected out there than in play areas used by the settled population, but their area of exploration is normally enclosed in the encampment and all the adults are aware of their presence. They can find concrete playgrounds with restrictions and set rules confusing and this can lead to misunderstandings with the adult supervisors.

Explain the playground rules and that the rules are there for everyone's safety. In one Hertfordshire school, lunchtime jobs are given to pupils as a reward. One popular job is to pick up litter. Two new Traveller pupils were given this treat and after a while the headteacher went out to check on them, only to discover them half way along the street collect-ing the litter. The children had not realised where the school boundary was. Notwithstanding such misunderstandings, children will feel in-cluded and good about themselves when they, like their classmates, do things for their school.

Large spaces can be intimidating. This is applicable to many pupils, so structured play activities could be provided for all children. Some schools have a policy whereby children can choose to stay in at lunch-time and attend indoor games, and this might benefit many children, including the Travellers.

Be alert to the possibility of name-calling and take immediate action, reporting it in line with the school's procedures. Children may expect hostility from adults as well as from the children and are unlikely to report such incidents unless actively encouraged to do so. If it is the

Traveller child who uses unacceptable language, a quiet explanation is better than a public reprimand.

Some of the pupils may be jealous about the newcomers if they feel they are receiving special treatment or see the incomers as a threat. They need to be reassured that their positions in the school hierarchy are not threatened and that they are not losing out. The playground, like the classroom, is an important arena to children and needs careful, sensitive management to ensure that it is a happy place for all the pupils.

Conclusion – only some of the questions

This is not a definitive list of suggestions nor a rulebook for others to follow. Neither is it a complete checklist of every issue and question that might arise. The theories and practice of education change constantly as we seek to improve the service we offer to pupils. What we have discovered, in consultation with schools, is that if a practice works for Traveller pupils it works for all pupils. So implementing the strategies indicated here will benefit not only Traveller children but all the children in the school.

7

Improving access to early educational opportunities for Traveller children

Kanta Wild-Smith

Working from a low baseline where Traveller children were starting school with two years less experience of non-family based education than many other children, Kanta Wild-Smith describes how innovative means such as play sacks, toddler talk, mobile libraries and family learning can be used to improve access for Travellers to early years settings.

Introduction and context

Essex is a large English shire county and has 58 primary, secondary and special schools. There is a relatively high population of Traveller families, as evidenced by the annual count by the Office of the Deputy Prime Minister and data collected by the Traveller Education Service (TES) and schools. It is difficult to collect precise statistics about numbers of Traveller families as there is no ethnic monitoring through the national Census, and many children are still not identified in the Pupil Level Annual Schools Census because of the families' fear of discrimination.

In 1997 the TES was funded to work only with statutory school age children and their schools. Then, as now, it focused on the most vulnerable and most mobile families, promoting access, attendance at school and achievement, raising awareness, working to avoid dependence on support services. A few Traveller parents did access pre-school provision independently but little support was available. Traveller parents often felt that up to the age of five or six education within the family was more appropriate. Many young Traveller children had never experienced separation from their parents or close extended family and for some parents this letting go of their child, to be cared for by somebody from another culture and in another place, was unthinkable. Parents had been subjected to discrimination and racism in the wider community and this frequently undermined their confidence in the state and its provision.

At that time the Early Years Development and Childcare Partnership (EYDCP) was beginning to co-ordinate provision, but funding arrangements and availability across localities was incomplete. The vision of nursery education for all three and four year olds whose parents wanted it was slowly becoming a reality. But the EYDCP lacked the information and support to aid Traveller parents in accessing provision in a situation where there were insufficient places in some areas and where parents were reluctant or poorly informed and some of whom were highly mobile and not literate.

The starting point – family learning

This was the situation in late 1998, when the Essex and Southend Consortium TES bid successfully for funding to support family learning – but not for pre-school, even though this seemed to us to be the most vital area to develop. But it did compel us to take a broad based approach to early learning.

Education in the early years is still a matter of parental choice, so we first approached the issue of access by looking at ways to inform parents of the benefits to their children of a quality pre-school experience. By working with parents to improve their knowledge and understanding of the skills and experiences young children need to develop, we hoped to broaden the home experience of the youngest Traveller children and raise the profile of learning through play. We also hoped that work in the early years would help smooth the eventual transition between home and school at age five.

Next moves – early years project workers

In April 1999 we appointed two project workers, whose original brief was complex and multi-faceted and who worked under the management of a senior TES teacher. The importance of having staff to focus specifically on development cannot be overstated. Though many useful contacts had been established before these two people were in post the existing staff had no time to follow contacts through effectively.

The original long-term objectives were to

- work with pre-schools, nurseries and health visitors to identify the needs and interests of Traveller parents and to encourage access to pre-school opportunities

- give Traveller parents a better understanding of the importance of learning through play

- promote access to SureStart programmes where available

- work closely with the Traveller Education Welfare Officer and teachers to identify suitable clients

- research into the level of need and interest in adult basic education

- liaise between Traveller families, schools and Adult and Community Education

- encourage access to school-based family learning programmes

A period of research ensued, and at the same time links were made with a network of professionals in health, early years and adult and community education and libraries. In four years we built up a framework for approaching family learning which met the objectives, and added other elements as appropriate. In particular we expanded our joint working with the library service and our training programme for early years staff and for staff of other departments and agencies. Incorporating both national and local initiatives as they came on stream, the family learning project developed along various paths.

A key development – Bookstart
In 1992 volunteers distributed picture books to babies in Birmingham at their eight-month health check. The parents were informed about how to access libraries and the importance to child development of sharing books with them. Findings from this longitudinal study were significant. Bookstart parents gave much higher priority to books than the control group; they visited libraries more often and initiated book sharing with their children more routinely.

In 1997 the Essex libraries Bookstart co-ordinator had contacted the TES to find out whether there was any on-going work to promote the Bookstart initiative to Traveller people, having been unable to find any initiatives in Bookstart nationally. Because some Traveller babies would miss the eight month health check and therefore not benefit from the scheme and because access to books for very young children was rare in the Traveller families, the Essex TES decided that Bookstart could be delivered to Traveller children up to the age of five in Essex. Family learning project workers trained as Bookstart volunteers and have since been able to deliver the Bookstart programme to the Traveller families who wanted it, in their homes. Essex Library Service has provided the books and materials in a partnership arrangement.

Some mothers said they didn't know that books designed specifically for very young children existed. Many parents related books only to formal reading in school and had had no experience of using them at home. Low levels of literacy amongst parents also meant that some mothers lacked the confidence to talk with their children about picture books. Delivering the Bookstart programme enabled the family learning workers to discuss literacy needs with the whole family and sparked off enquiries about pre-school and adult basic education. Between September 1999 and April 2002 the TES made over 270 Bookstart visits, including visits to highly mobile families at the roadside, who might not have managed to access any other form of education for their children. The partnership with the Bookstart programme has been invaluable in providing a first, positive contact with families and a foundation on which to build parental knowledge of other early years educational opportunities.

Linking into the Early Years Development and Childcare Partnership

The work of the TES was recognised at an early stage through inclusion in the county Child-care Strategy Plan. The family learning project manager also sat on a county-wide equal opportunities working party which has since become a standing advisory group to the Partnership. This working party produced a manual of good practice in equal opportunities in the early years called *A World of Opportunities: a working guide to equal opportunities in practice* (Essex County Council, 2001) which includes a section on working with Traveller children and their families. This manual was distributed free of charge to all Essex settings and is continually being updated.

This link of early years work to the mainstream within the authority has been invaluable. The support of the EYDCP became evident in increased networking with other practitioners, leading to better access to funding opportunities, both for families in settings and for TES inspired initiatives such as Play Sacks. It has enabled the work of the TES to be in the mainstream of early years and child-care developments in a way that had been virtually impossible before. The link also meant the family learning project workers could provide staff in settings with accurate and up to date information.

Further developments – Play Sacks and Toddler Talk

Building on the Bookstart programme and on the use of Play Boxes, the West Midlands Consortium Education Service for Travelling Children thought that parents required information, advice and equipment that demonstrated the value of learning through play. Few parents understood the links between early learning, pre-school education and the reading and writing skills that they wanted their children to acquire. Lack of space in some homes also meant that although outdoor toys were available parents purchased little indoor play equipment and wanted advice on toys which have good play and educational value that could be stored in a small space.

With the help of an access grant from the EYDCP, the TES purchased suitable educational toys and had specially produced storage bags made to lend parents. The aim was to increase access to mainstream early years settings by developing parents' understanding of the value of learning through play. Parents could also borrow indoor toys for approximately three weeks at a time. A Play Sack was specifically designed for each child, on a theme relating to the early learning goals in the Foundation Stage of the National Curriculum and was delivered and explained to the parents, who in turn introduced their children to the activities around the toys.

Some parents enjoyed playing and experimenting with the contents of the Play Sacks themselves, as they hadn't experienced activities like cutting and sticking when they were children. When the contents of the Play Sacks are changed some three weeks later, they are first evaluated for their suitability. A few parents were worried about the responsibility entailed by borrowing the toys, even though we tried to reassure them. Servicing the Play Sacks takes a good deal of staff time and it would be good if it were done by dedicated workers. New local SureStart programmes and one school have taken up the idea, so more parents and children have access to such resources.

When we were delivering Play Sacks we could see that they contained nothing suitable for one and two year olds. Some of the Play Sacks equipment was unsuitable for their use. We used a further access grant from the EYDCP for our Toddler Talk initiative in 2001, designed to aid the development of speaking and listening skills in babies and toddlers. One parent who was loaned a child's tape player with nursery rhymes and story tapes was so impressed by her son's interest and enjoyment that she promptly bought him his own little collection. We also noted how older children enjoyed playing and learning with their youngest siblings' tapes.

The Play Sacks and Toddler Talk initiatives both illustrate the importance of learning through play for child development, without undermining the parents' role as first and prime educator of their children. The contents of each sack are carefully chosen. The equipment is age specific but the age of other family members needs to be taken into account for safety reasons. Some parents have objected to certain toys on gender grounds – maintaining, for instance, that kitchen equipment is only for girls – and this can need sensitive explanation and handling. That some items will be lost has to be accepted or parents will be afraid to borrow things, but in fact few resources are damaged or mislaid.

Accessing early years settings

We knew few Traveller children who had attended a pre-school setting in Essex in 1997. Most started school at age five or later, with no experience of ever being separated from their family. So Traveller children were starting school with two years less experience of non-family based education than many other children. This affected their access to the Foundation Stage and the early years curriculum.

Raising the profile of learning through play by means of Bookstart, Play Sacks and Toddler Talk, and supporting visits to playgroups and nurseries, has given more of the mothers confidence in early years settings to look after their children for part of the day. Travellers opted mostly for local pre-school playgroups in Essex rather than school-based nurseries, partly by choice and partly because of proximity. Factors that have inhibited access have been lack of transport, mobility and their personal feelings about their duty and traditions of raising children.

As a matter of policy, Essex has avoided setting up pre-schools on the twelve county council owned caravan sites, preferring instead to encourage parents to use the local nursery settings. This has fostered Travellers' contact with the local community and has afforded most parents a choice of several settings with high quality provision.

Staff training

Pre-school staff, like primary and secondary school teachers, may know little about Traveller cultures and lifestyles and have low expectations of Traveller children, so recognise their need for training. The family learning project team have delivered formal and informal training to early years staff and students, health professionals, librarians and others. An information leaflet produced by the TES is distributed as part of the training. Understanding more about Traveller children's culture, lifestyles and experiences helps staff to create a welcoming environment. For example, it is important for Traveller children to see their own culture reflected in the stories read to them. Play caravans or a home corner set out as a caravan interior will delight all the children.

However good the training, the best way for staff to increase their knowledge and skills is through positive relationships with Traveller parents and children – another reason to favour access to existing mainstream early years settings rather than separate provision. With sensitive handling, the whole community can benefit from increased social contact.

Although Traveller children are by no means all disadvantaged in the usual meaning of the word, many of their parents have suffered social exclusion and discrimination. Children witness such hostility from early in their lives. The Effective Provision of Pre School Education (EPPE) Research Project (Sylva *et al*, 2003) found that disadvantaged children do better in settings with a mixture of children from a range of social backgrounds rather than being kept together. This has implications for the siting of settings.

The mobile library project, Education on Wheels

The involvement of Essex libraries in the Bookstart initiative has led the TES to work in partnership to make mobile libraries more accessible to Travellers. Some librarians were apprehensive, basing their views of Travellers on negative media coverage, so training was given to all the mobile librarians. Routes were scrutinised to see where stops could be made at the county council and the larger private caravan sites.

Librarians worked with the TES to identify resources with particular appeal for Travellers of all ages to add to their stock. They now carry photograph collections of Traveller horse fairs, history books and books about animals, pictures and storybooks of the kind listed in the resources at the end of this book. The books and also videos have proved extremely popular and some families have purchased their own copies of books they particularly enjoyed.

The TES also agreed to provide a member of staff to support the mobile librarian at first, as many of the new borrowers needed help in joining the library or in finding what they wanted. The support worker read stories to some of the children and let them practice their own reading. Links with local settings also meant that in some cases children were encouraged to bring in the book they had borrowed to share.

The Education on Wheels project had such an impact that many families began to use a library for the first time and became confident to use local branch libraries. The Essex library service increased its stock of Traveller heritage books and has recently used its grant from the Children's Fund to employ a dedicated worker to expand the Traveller children's use of mobile libraries.

Family learning projects in schools

Just when the TES project started, Essex County Council was actively promoting family learning projects in schools, linking with the County Co-ordinator and family learning tutors, through meetings and attendance at their termly conference. The focus of family learning was then on particular year groups of children or parents who had left school with few formal qualifications. The Traveller parents known to our Service often needed basic help with their literacy and were uncomfortable among parents with full schooling behind them. They were further excluded because these classes were advertised by sending leaflets from school.

The TES family learning project raised awareness of the needs of the Traveller parents with schools and tutors. Classes for the parents of the youngest children in one school combining basic First Aid tuition with talks about reading and writing were a great success. The parents also spent time in the children's classes and school assemblies. The intention was to move on to adult basic education classes at the school, but too many of the families moved on. Valuable lessons were learned, though. These parents showed us that there was a need

▓ to approach parents individually and talk face to face to secure their interest

▓ for an outreach worker who can also attend the class to support those parents with no school experience

▓ for flexibility over the attendance of adults unaccustomed to regular commitment to a class and who have heavy family obligations

There are clearly huge potential benefits to parents and children who are settled enough to attend an eight or ten week course. The sight of the children's faces when they saw their parents in class and assembly, and the parents' pleasure at sharing their children's day was hugely rewarding.

Family learning workers in Essex have supported adult Travellers who wished to attend evening basic skills classes. Both the project workers completed the volunteers' course for adult learners, but it became clear that additional staff were needed, as the classes took up so much time. It would be sad if the lessons were dropped, as Traveller parents told us that the experience of their children starting school and beginning to learn to read has motivated them to learn as well, so they can help their children with their learning.

Conclusion

The EPPE Project (Sylva *et al*, 2003) index to measure the quality of the home learning environment shows that what parents and carers do makes a real difference to young children's development. The index measured a range of activities parents undertake with pre-school children that relate to improvements in children's learning and development. These are activities of the kind supported through the Toddler Talk and Play Sacks projects such as: sharing books with children, teaching songs and rhymes, painting and drawing, playing with letters and numbers, visiting the library and teaching alphabet and number. Taking children for visits and encouraging regular play with others at home also significantly promote learning opportunities.

All parents want the best for their children. Where children have had successful experience of learning through play at home, and their parents are supported to understand why this is so vital to their child's development, the transition to another place of learning – playgroup or school – becomes more acceptable. By setting our early years work firmly in the wider context of family learning, we have benefited the whole family. And by encouraging Traveller parents to access local pre-school settings for their children has been good for the whole community.

8

It's all about me – resources at Foundation and Key Stage 1

Lorna Daymond

This chapter rehearses the importance of culturally relevant resources for Traveller pupils. Lorna Daymond relates how one TES went about addressing the dearth of such resources, principally with the ground breaking fiction book Sean's Wellies *and illustrates how such resources can be used in the classroom at Foundation and Key Stage 1.*

The Traveller child's world

On a Traveller site, much of the children's play so vital for learning, takes place outside the trailer. The environment and the toys bought by Travellers often favour the development of gross motor skills and a sense of space. Few families appear to buy or use paint, crayons, Playdoh or plasticine, glue or scissors to develop fine motor skills. There is little space in the all-purpose rooms of the trailer for experimenting with materials of this kind. Most Traveller children learn by being actively engaged in activities, by doing rather than by narrative, instruction and planning. Children may be bought videos to watch, but though these may entertain they do not require a response or interaction. Adult conversation may be continuous around them, from which they are neither excluded nor included. Functional literacy to interpret formal documents may not be present in the family. Few commercially marketed toys or games reflect the Traveller lifestyle. Travellers, by and large, comply with and accept the commercial toy market, but the commercial market does not reflect or engage with them and the few toys Traveller families purchase are rarely those which support literacy.

The lack of cultural acceptance and reflection may be one reason why Traveller parents have been reluctant to access pre-school provision – they feel that 'all this has very little to do with people like us'. Although there is now strong evidence to suggest that an increasing number of Traveller children are accessing some form of pre-school provision, many practical barriers remain. Teachers and providers at Foundation Stage or Key Stage 1 should ask themselves: To what extent are we, the settled community, recognising and meeting Traveller children's interests and preferred learning styles? What shared language is there between the home environment and school? What understanding does the playgroup leader, the nursery or class teacher have of Traveller children's everyday life and surroundings? How far has the setting or school reached out to the Travellers' world instead of expecting Travellers to comply with the interests and pre-occupations of the settled community?

Starting school – the chase to catch up

By the time they start school, some Traveller children already appear to have a low starting point in numeracy and literacy. Learning is closely tied to the learner's culture. Jean Conteh (2003) observes that how we each use language is shaped by our background and environment. When Traveller children start school, their teachers' use of language may seem new and strange to them. The children may be puzzled by what they learn, how they are expected to learn it, and why they are learning it. Should their parents have experienced limited schooling themselves, they may be just as puzzled. As children progress through the school, the language becomes more specialised and remote from that used at home. Their specific knowledge and skills may count for nothing, the subjects of study do not relate to the priorities of home life and they have no power to decide what counts as useful knowledge in the school situation.

> They have to learn to write answers to questions, rather than say them ('and usually in complete sentences'), to fill in blanks, to write instructions for other people, to report on things they have done, to summarise ideas from text, to write lists of correctly-spelt words ... the list goes on and on. (Conteh, 2003)

Small wonder that too many Traveller children drop out of schooling at the stage of transfer to secondary school. The reasons for this are many and complex but one has to do with how they feel they can engage with the language, culture and curriculum of the classroom. If Traveller pupils are to feel that their time at school is benefiting them, they must feel they can be themselves and have their identity acknowledged and respected. There needs to be some cross-cultural area in which they and their teachers can talk on equal terms, where they share a common language. It is now widely accepted that:

> Where the presence of travelling children is openly acknowledged, and where accurate and positive images of the different nomadic communities are featured within both the resources of the school and the curriculum, then the response is lively and there is genuine openness to learning. (Ofsted, 1996)

Producing resources – finding the Traveller story
Some fifteen years ago, a search for books about Travellers would have revealed few written for young children. With notable exceptions, most children's stories portrayed Gypsy or Irish Travellers in a negative light or were hopelessly romantic. There were the standard images and products relating to fairs and circuses, but scant culturally reflective games or resources. When we, as a Traveller Education Service (TES) enquired as to why this was so, manufacturers explained that the market was too limited, that it would not be commercially viable. Frustrated by this lack of resources, we began to take photographs in an amateur fashion, to take advantage of chemists and photographic suppliers who offered a jigsaw-making service from customers' photographs. Those jigsaws, despite the inappropriate number of pieces – it was 100 or nothing – were the beginning of our making culturally reflective resources.

It was Dodie, a young Scottish Traveller lad who first gave us the idea of producing a book. When he was a baby, his story-telling family had given him a story of his own. He mentioned this to one of our TES advisory support teachers and she suggested that he might like to write the story down. It proved to be quite a long tale, and slightly outside his written language ability. So she wrote it for him, and the beginnings of *Silly Jake* were born. An officer in the local education authority suggested that a teacher who had been producing resources for them might be interested in illustrating the story, and he did so. The book, with black and white illustrations and printed by the LEA on glossy paper, was launched by the Chief Education Officer at a small gathering in the local teachers' centre. Dodie's family was delighted. This was a book that related to them, to their family, to their son.

The story continues

Surprised and pleased with the positive response to *Silly Jake*, we began to consider other options. We had made a video, *A Close Knit Community*, part of which showed Appleby Fair and thought another visit to Appleby might provide useful material for books. To keep costs down, we worked from photographs that we took inexpertly, and put together the texts for *Counting Book 1* and *Counting Book 2*. The Education Advisory Service printed them in 1993, funded by the TES. Despite the books' limitations – we were unhappy with the formation of some of the 1-10 figures – they were enthusiastically received by the Traveller community, especially by the families who saw themselves or their relatives in the photographs. Individual children in school would say 'That's Uncle Billy' or 'We've got cushions like that', and engage with the books. These initial responses encapsulate the key elements of culturally specific resources. At last, Traveller children and their families can see themselves in the resources being used in the world outside their own environment.

Two talk-about books, *Travellers at Fairs and Festivals* and *Families at Appleby Fair* followed in 1994, using the same format of photograph with short text above and related question below. Aware that our publications had focused on the traditional Traveller communities, in the same year we produced *Amber and Annie*, a counting book featuring two small New Traveller girls. Members of encampment were extremely helpful in setting up photo opportunities and suggesting ideas for particular numbers, especially the larger ones up to 10. The girls' families showed tremendous trust and self-confidence, as the photographs were to identify *Amber and Annie* and their mother as New Travellers for all time. Not surprisingly, *Amber and Annie* didn't sell as many copies, but that didn't matter; what mattered was that we had a book to which children from New Traveller communities could relate. It endorsed the fact that we as a TES were New Traveller friendly. Also, the Norfolk schools Amber and Annie attended could use the book in classes, and that in some way authenticated to other pupils that the girls were part of the wider community and had status as such.

Finding our feet – *Shaun's Wellies*

What we had produced until then might appeal to the visual or auditory learner, but had little to offer kinaesthetic learners. In 1995 Sue, a teacher on secondment from a local infant school, produced a series of draft sketches of her ideas, with a text appropriate for Reception and Year 1 and illustrations with lift-up flaps.

The story was about a situation common to any child, the temporary mislaying of an item of clothing or equipment, in this case a pair of Wellington boots, and the search to find them. As photographs would be inappropriate, we consulted the LEA Advisory Service design section to find a suitable professional artist. He turned out to be skilled at portraying wildlife; we used this skill and his ideas by incorporating a snail into many of the pictures as a continuous theme separate from the story but providing something for readers to search for as they turned the pages. The artist met and drew a group of Traveller children from a local site. The main character in the book was based on a real lad called Shaun, who had been attending Sue's school. Paintings rather than photographs rendered the illustrations one step away from reality. So for the book to have credibility with the Traveller population, the pictures had to be accurate in every detail. Accordingly, several site visits were made to ensure that the caravans that the illustrator was to paint really looked like Traveller trailers, that the door was depicted on the correct side, that the churns were properly placed and the internal layout of the trailer correct.

The illustrations and the printing of *Shaun's Wellies* were done in two parts, the main images being on separate sheets from the flaps, which had to marry up exactly when they were hand-assembled and glued. The cost for the initial print run of 1,000 was over £6,700. By selling copies at £6.95 each we managed to break even. The County INSET Centre was responsible for overseeing the design and a small, local and efficient publisher printed the books. Schools and TESs were soon asking whether there was an A2 big book sized version. We tentatively ordered this, with an initial print run of 200. The format for both books was landscape. This was fine for the A4 version but rendered the spirally bound A2 copies rather cumbersome for class teachers to hold, and slightly too large for the big book stands. The success of both versions is proven by the A4 version having been reprinted three times and the big books twice, with sales to libraries and private bookshops across the UK.

The growth of Traveller specific resources

At about the same time, Wiltshire TES produced *A Horse for Joe*, an attractive full colour storybook illustrated with photographs and original watercolours. The tale of Joe, who dreams of owning a horse, is told at two levels, with a caption line for less confident readers. Photocopiable activity sheets relating to Key Stages 1 and 2 of the national curriculum accompanied the book. Other TESs began to devise and publish their own material, among which were *Monday Morning*, from Hertfordshire Traveller Education Project, with full colour photographs and available in three sizes. Written by Sandy Madden and produced by the Avon Consortium TES, *Melissa to the Rescue* has flaps and moving parts and over 55 words from the national curriculum Key Stage 1 first list of high frequency words. Suddenly books were becoming available that depicted Traveller life as a natural background to a main story. TESs were providing exciting extension materials and story sacks, based either on their own books or, with due regard to copyright, the books from other TESs.

Responding to requests for a follow-up version to *Shaun's Wellies* Norfolk TES produced *Ruby's Rabbits* in 2002, using the same illustrator but having a more traditional portrait format. The text, aimed at Year 1 pupils, consists of a short question relating to the picture, and a one-sentence answer. As before, the artist based his characters – including the rabbit – on a real family and we were careful to check everything with them. Some compromises had to be made: the flapped front door of Granny's house had to open outwards to allow the reader to lift it and reveal Granny behind it. Responding to schools' requests, we produced a big book version for whole-class reading and a curriculum guide that suggested ideas for using *Ruby's Rabbits* as the focus for cross-curricular activities and learning.

Three dimensional resources

But what of young Traveller children who remain resistant to books or text-related activities? In an attempt to engage all children while also attracting Traveller children in imaginative play, speaking and listening, we commissioned a local craftsman to work for two weeks on producing plans for small and robust caravans that closely resembled a Roma trailer, inside and out. He took photographs, contacted trailer manufacturers, drew scaled plans and produced his first model several months later. Other TESs now buy these trailers and, perhaps more importantly, so do pre-schools and schools for all their children.

Using the resources in the classroom

Most Traveller children, like all children, prefer to read and write about something that interests them and to which they can relate. John's response to the Traveller materials vividly illustrates how positive culturally reflective resources can be. Eight year old John missed several years of schooling because he started late. His parents have limited literacy and little space at home is given over to books, reading or writing. John has an intense interest in, and knowledge of, chickens – and very little else. Presented with *Literacy Trail*, a culturally specific literacy scheme that is successful in encouraging many Traveller children to read and write, he showed no interest whatever. His TES advisory support teacher, who sees him for an hour twice a week, tried valiantly to engage him in a range of materials, to no avail. She devised various materials specifically for him but, with all the goodwill in the world, it is hard to deliver the entire curriculum based on chickens.

The breakthrough came in June with *A Horse for Joe*. John had just returned from Appleby Fair, the setting for the book, and he began to talk to the advisory support teacher about his experiences there. It emerged that his grandfather bred horses. After reading *A Horse for Joe* together many times, John's teacher photocopied the pictures and drew a horizontal line under each. With her help, John, still at the CVC stage of reading and word building, was able to write a simple sentence under each picture to retell the story. He moved on to *Melissa to the Rescue*. After reading the book slowly and carefully together and enjoying the moving parts, John's teacher once again photocopied the pictures, cut round each of the characters, word-processed the key words (Melissa, rope, water, foal, horse), stuck them onto the images, and laminated each image with the word. John was able to sequence these with the aid of sentence strips. He could read four simple sentences headed 'How to warm up a foal'. Given a few simple ClipArt images, each labelled with the key word such as 'handle', 'wheel', 'lift', 'push', he was able to compose and write his own sentences on 'How to use a wheelbarrow'.

The small-scale play trailers were an instant success. It was interesting to listen to young children in a setting deciding where the cooker and fridge should go or how the bed folded down. In an inner-city nursery class that was known to have one housed Traveller, it was fascinating to hear two other children volunteer that 'my Gran used to live in one of those, but she's in a house now'. Even more unexpected was how boys of middle junior school age were happy to play with it, whereas they would have spurned a dolls' house. A trailer is different: it has wheels, it has man-appeal.

The big books already referred to are a useful addition to whole-class reading resources. Not only do they help Traveller children to engage but they also offer all children knowledge and understanding, an implied acceptance of Traveller lifestyle as being valid and legal, and the opportunity for children to question and comment and for the teacher to deal positively and factually with any inappropriate remarks.

Many culturally specific resources can be easily and cheaply purchased at Traveller horse fairs. Over the last few years, our team has collected, among much else, a set of blue and white plastic bowls and jugs, traditional style pegs made from wood with binding strips of aluminium, stainless steel water churns, Haddon Hall china plates, cups and saucers, beautifully decorated cushions, soft minky baby blankets, a lilac satin cot cover with silver lace and embroidered with the shape of two dummies, aprons, children's clothes worn on special occasions, including exquisite bibs elaborately decorated with lace and gold thread, and various items of tack for horses.

Working with teachers during a training session, we explored how these resources might be used, along with books and photographs, in the Foundation and Key Stage 1 curriculum. The ideas were endless. The elaborate dresses and baby wear are an excellent starting point for investigation around the class about what each child might wear on special occasions, how in society we use particular clothing for particular activities or for particular events. And there is plenty of scope for dressing up and role-play. The china can lead to investigation into pattern, what different communities use as plates – leaves, wood, metal, paper, fired clay – designing a plate, or considering when 'best' china is used, for whom and what its use signifies.

The churns, bowl and jug lend themselves to exploration of volume and weight as well as different materials for different uses ('What would happen if we tried to cook using the plastic bowl?') and domestic role-play. The pegs are used within creative development ('Remember peg dolls?'), design and technology and mathematics ('How many pegs can you put on the line before the egg timer runs out?'), as well as role-play.

All the resources can be utilised in some way within citizenship and PSHE. They involve Traveller pupils in a meaningful way and widen the knowledge and understanding of the whole class.

Conclusion

The importance of having cultural acknowledgement and representation throughout the curriculum has been stressed by HMI, Ofsted, academics and informed practitioners. Nevertheless it would be difficult, and unethical, to prove this by artificially setting up a control group that was deliberately denied any reference to their culture and identity. It is possible however, to point to strong circumstantial evidence and draw reasonable conclusions by comparing the attendance, achievement and inclusion data in the schools that demonstrate such good practice with similar data from those reticent about acknowledging and reflecting Traveller backgrounds.

Although there is no national annual data on the attainment of Traveller pupils, the collated data from thirteen LEAs in the Eastern Region of England[1] shows a marked increase in attainment in the end of key stage tests in Maths and English between 1999/00, when regional benchmarking began, and 2001/02. Teachers will have seen for themselves the increase in self-esteem on the part of the Traveller children in their schools and the increase in knowledge and understanding of other pupils when the curriculum is made inclusive of Travellers.

Perhaps the most valuable endorsements come from the Traveller families themselves. A Year 1 teacher reported that Freddy was not interested in reading until he saw pictures in one of the class books of trailers on a site. He immediately perked up and said:

'I live in one of those. What does it say about them? Read it to me.'

Having suffered considerable discrimination all her life, a Traveller mother expressed her approval of one book produced by a TES and encouraged its use in class, saying:

'Let them see we're just like everyone else.'

And then there is Peggy, fair-haired and blue-eyed, who looked in amazement at *Monday Morning*, and said:

'I want to read that book – it's got *me* in it.'

The development of culturally based resources has focused on all aspects of literacy, including the all-important area of speaking and listening, an area in which some Travellers and teachers feel less than confident. Many Traveller adults confidently apply mathematics and science in their everyday lives. Perhaps we need to be questioning whether there needs to be cultural references and resources within those areas of the curriculum too.

Note
1 Norfolk, Essex and Southend, Suffolk, Bedfordshire, Hertfordshire, Northants., Leicestershire, Leicester City, Cambridgeshire, Havering, Luton, Peterborough, Lincolnshire

9

'Literacy for All' and other curriculum partnerships at Key Stage 2

Margaret Wood

Cambridgeshire's largest ethnic minority group are Travellers. 'Literacy for All' is a project to raise Traveller pupil attainment within the context of raising ethnic minority pupil achievement. Margaret Wood offers a guide to the use of Key Stage 2 Traveller specific texts in case study examples and proves how the impetus for Traveller specific work can act on a broad front, raising the profile of inclusion across a large county.

The Cambridgeshire context and challenge

Cambridgeshire has a large and diverse Traveller population. The majority are traditional Gypsy or Romany Travellers. There are increasing numbers of Irish Travellers and Showmen, many based on their own land, and smaller numbers from Scottish, Welsh, New Traveller and Circus backgrounds. There are twelve local authority sites, mainly in rural areas, but more Travellers live on private sites, some very large and some without planning permission. The team for Traveller Education also supports increasing numbers of children whose families have moved into housing, often temporarily and as a last resort. There is a steady flow of Travellers living for short periods of time on unauthorised stopping places. Some, but by no means all, of the children attend local schools while they are with us, so lack of access to education is still a serious concern.

An important challenge for the Traveller Education team is to help the LEA to enable schools to respond to the varied needs of the whole school population, including Travellers. Even where schools have considerable experience of working with Traveller pupils, many of the mainstream teachers and Learning Support Assistants (LSAs) do not feel confident about working with Travellers. Traveller pupils have significantly lower than average levels of attainment. This cannot be ignored, particularly in a county like Cambridgeshire where Gypsy and Irish Travellers are the largest ethnic minority group in certain areas.

Meeting the challenge – a shared commitment

Clearly, the Traveller Education team cannot take sole responsibility for the education of all Traveller pupils on and off school rolls. A relatively small team cannot single-handedly address the many challenging issues such as access, interrupted schooling, late starts, tackling racism and prejudice, low literacy levels and secondary transfer. For us to work towards the goal of genuine equality of outcome for Travellers requires a shared commitment and consistent approach right across schools and the LEA.

In our authority, the Race Equality and Diversity Service (within which, the Traveller Education Service is organised) has a high profile. LEA structures allow us to have a significant influence on the other LEA services, without whom progress cannot be made. Our whole ethos depends on establishing partnerships with inspectors, advisors, headteachers, Education Welfare and all the other Pupil Support Services. Travellers are an important priority in the Education Development Plan. LEA policy and planning increasingly take account of their needs. If Cambridgeshire is to raise attainment overall, then it has to raise the attainment of Travellers.

Literacy for All – the beginnings

When the National Literacy Strategy was introduced, we recognised its potential importance for Traveller children in schools. We made sure that all our staff received the appropriate training. Representatives of our service spent time with the Literacy Team discussing how we could jointly support schools with Traveller, Black and bilingual pupils. For some time, there was little or no guidance provided nationally, so we worked with one another on how to inform staff in schools in our area. During this period, as usually happens with new initiatives, we developed our thinking through regular liaison with Traveller Education colleagues across the country. Not surprisingly, few books were available that lent themselves to the demands of the literacy hour. However, many Traveller Education Services were quick to produce big books and other materials of such high quality that they can be used by whole classes side by side with resources from mainstream publishers.

Literacy for All is a jointly co-ordinated, collaborative project involving staff from the Race Equality and Diversity Service, a literacy consultant from the advisory service and mainstream colleagues in primary schools. A literacy consultant had time specifically allocated to work closely with me and an advisory teacher. At our initial meeting we discussed how support staff raise attainment by providing effective input in the literacy hour. Some of our colleagues felt that their time was being wasted for parts of the lesson. Some mainstream teachers did not know how to plan for the varied needs of the whole class and asked for pupils to be withdrawn. Some Traveller pupils had poor literacy because of interrupted schooling. This was aggravated by the irrelevance to them of the texts they were asked to read. We wanted to work with a group of teachers to try to make improvements, to share good practice and work towards long-term solutions.

The stated aims of *Literacy for All* were:

- to develop good working practice in schools working with Traveller, Black and bilingual children
- to share good practice with all schools
- to focus on linking the teaching of writing to the teaching of reading
- to focus on improving writing

Staff worked together in pairs to plan and deliver weekly literacy plans based on texts that, although particularly suitable for supporting our target children, were suitable for all children and could be used in all schools.

The first step was to motivate staff and schools. We drew up a list of schools with whom our staff had already built positive relationships. We decided that the project would have more status with schools if it were endorsed by the literacy team, so the consultant phoned headteachers just before we sent out letters inviting them to attend a launch meeting with one mainstream and one service member of staff. We hoped to publish sample schemes of work for the literacy hour for all years from reception to Year Six and for three terms. The materials had to be suitable for classes including Traveller, Black and bilingual pupils and, as far as possible, use texts which reflect a range of cultures. The materials would then be collated and published. We presented this as an exciting opportunity for us to work in a more equal partnership with mainstream staff. Twelve schools signed up to the project at the first meeting.

We met in one of the participating primary schools. Our LEA is so large that some teachers find it hard to visit our base. Many were overwhelmed by the range and quality of culturally diverse resources that we put on display. Everyone was given a support pack containing lists of relevant books and other materials and advice on evaluating books suitable for use with our target group. We also gave everyone a disk containing a planning grid on which to record their weekly plans, which then had to be sent to the literacy consultant for collation.

Project mechanics – 'The Traveller child in the class came to life'

Staff were asked to plan and teach one unit of work per term and to produce short-term plans and any accompanying resources such as games, puppets and worksheets. The plan would include opportunities for using the child's first language, including Romanes where appropriate. It would include speaking and listening activities and have visual outcomes, for example a story map. There also had to be a focus on addressing inclusion issues. Above all, we asked everyone to try to provide a good practice model for other schools, both in terms of literacy teaching, and in the ways colleagues and support staff could work together to provide a lively interactive style of teaching that would engage all children.

At the launch meeting we highlighted aspects of the National Literacy Strategy that would be most relevant for this project. The packs included detailed guidance on preparing a unit of work, which was presented to the group by the literacy consultant. An example of the guidance appears in Appendix 2. We showed examples of good practice from the guidance on *Supporting Pupils learning English as an Additional Language* (DfES, 1999) and talked through issues specific to Traveller pupils.

The literacy consultant had recently observed a lesson taught by two of the Key Stage 1 participants and they were invited to describe their first experience of joint planning and teaching. Their enthusiasm and excitement about their first three lessons using *Melissa to the Rescue* (Madden, 1999) were inspiring. The Traveller child in the class had come to life. He had words and knowledge he could share with the rest of the class, and it was all part of the lesson for everyone. The rest of our group were keen to go away and make a start. As the project progressed, other colleagues reported noticing delight and recognition on the faces of Traveller pupils. For example in a Key Stage 2 lesson using *A Horse for Joe* (Hird and Whitwell, 1999) one boy volunteered proudly, 'I'm a Gypsy, Miss!'

Some of the texts chosen for Key Stage 2 included *Snowy* (Doherty, 1992), *Fireside Tales of the Traveller Children* (Williamson, 1993), *Get it Sorted* (Devon Traveller Education Service, 1998), *Plaits and Braids* (Cambridgeshire Multicultural Education Service, 2002) and *Stone Soup* (Williams, 1999). Some of the *Plaits and Braids* lessons included extracts from *Girl in Red* (Hicyilmaz, 2000) and more recently colleagues have used *My Gran* (Parker, 1999), *A Moving Way of Life* (Cunningham, 1997) and Ewan MacColl's *The Moving On Song*. On visits to observe *Literacy for All* lessons, it was clear from discussions with headteachers and at the project meetings that joint planning and delivery of the lessons had given added value and often proved inspirational for pupils and teachers alike.

Evaluation

We identified the following evidence of success, particularly with the Traveller pupils:

- pupils were enthusiastic, engaged and able to identify with the resources and/or activities

- pupils were more confident and showed higher self-esteem

- there was a focus on pupils' learning needs and so teaching was more coherent

- literacy improved

- pupil relationships improved as social skills developed through children's newly acquired vocabulary to talk about relationships

- resources and activities which highlight diversity endorsed pupils' right to be different

- improved pupil behaviour and more sustained concentration

In our evaluation we tried to consider qualitative and quantitative data – evidence of pupils' work, teacher assessments and Standard Assessment Tests (SATs). It is difficult to measure the direct impact of a project such as this on SATs results, but as most teachers reported improved motivation, this is bound to affect pupils' test results.

The Individual Education Plans of children with individual educational needs were consulted for planning differentiated tasks and activities and to inform grouping for small group work.

We discussed the benefits of the project for all children and came up with the following:

- the close involvement of the literacy consultant whose team trains all schools

- two adults working together give pupils a positive role model of collaboration. This makes the literacy hour more vibrant and the strategy can be extended to whole-school activities

- teachers have a better chance to try something different and become more adventurous

- staff model being learners themselves

- the class teacher has time to work with different groups of children and to observe them learning

- the class sees the support teacher as the whole class lead teacher and vice versa

- an easier text enables pupils to undertake more complicated tasks

- children experience a greater variety of texts

- diversity became respected and appreciated

- the pupils' empathy and awareness was raised

- working with a different (additional) adult enhanced learning

One of the longer-term outcomes was that a number of mainstream teachers enjoyed the role change and the joint planning, saying they would like to work in this way in the future.

Obstacles to collaborative work

There can be obstacles to working so closely with mainstream teachers especially when peripatetic staff might only be in the school once a week. The support staff found different solutions depending on the circumstances. Increasingly, the headteachers who understand the benefits of joint working have made planning time available, often by teaching a class themselves to provide release time. Some of the units were jointly planned but taught only by one or other of the partners, at least on some days. In some cases, our staff rearranged their timetables for the *Literacy for All* weeks so they could be fully involved. In one school, the project was taught on one day each week instead of over two weeks as usual.

Beyond literacy – Traveller culture across the curriculum

The use of the *Literacy for All* project acted as a stimulus for specific projects undertaken at Key Stage 2 across a variety of curriculum areas.

A year 3/4 class worked on *The Broken Broomstick* (Taylor, 1999). The teachers planned and taught jointly, using a text featuring Traveller culture. The TES teacher felt that joint planning contributed to well-focused and active lesson content and the class teacher reported that she had learned a great deal from the lessons. Even though the school always has Traveller pupils, the teamwork approach had enabled her to learn more.

In another school, the TES teacher planned and taught a two week sequence of lessons for a year 3/4 class based on the story *Night of Peace* from *Fireside Tales of the Traveller Children* (Williamson, 1993). The class responded well to the use of drama and play scripts and the project was repeated in another school the following year. The dramatised version of the story became a class assembly, raising the profile of the work and of Travellers in the whole school.

In a Year 5/6 class the work was based upon *The Travelling People* (Wormington, Newman and Lilly, 2000), using the big book and a set of pupil books and focusing on note taking and report writing. This enabled the Traveller teacher and the class teacher to cooperate by face-to-face meetings and e-mail correspondence. A great deal of information about Travellers was passed on to pupils through this non-fiction book and affirmed the two Traveller pupils in the class, who were able to contribute information from their own knowledge and experience.

A mixed Year 2/3 class used *Traveller Alphabet* (Essex County Council, 1995) over two weeks. The class teacher is interested in languages and was keen to develop phonic skills by reading unfamiliar words. The non-Traveller pupils were fascinated by a visit by Traveller poet Kathleen Cunningham, who talked about the Romany language first hand. The whole class was motivated by the task of producing their own book. Making books, individually or in groups and often in interesting formats, has been a popular feature of the whole project. In this school there was contact with a Traveller parent who was initially antagonistic about the school teaching children the Romany language. She was duly reassured and then brought in a book about Travellers her family owned and this brought her children to positive attention in the class.

In a Year 4 class the teachers used *Children of Britain Just Like Me* (Kindersley *et al*, 1999). The pupils looked at organisational features of non-fiction such as captions, photographs and page layout. They examined the content of the book and focused on a selection of children from different ethnic backgrounds including Sara Lee, a Gypsy, and her family. The children used a digital camera and a word processor to write a caption under a picture of themselves. They were asked to copy some features of page layout and went on to write a page about themselves in the third person in the style of the book. Traveller children in the class were confident enough of themselves to write about their homes, families and lifestyles and some of them drew horses and trailers.

Year 5 children who used Kit Wright's poem, *The Magic Box*, as a stimulus for their own poetry, wrote about boxing, horse riding and their families. When a year 3 class read *Stone Soup* (*Ibid*, 1999), Travellers proudly revealed their ethnicity to the group and to a visiting adult, and some other children reported their Traveller connections. Year 6 pupils with Special Educational Needs used *My Gran* (*Ibid*, 1999) as an example of biographical writing and were interested to investigate family names and their derivations as a spin off.

A Year 3 art project aimed to explore patterns and the TES teacher helped plan lessons on the theme of Crown Derby plates. The children spent ten minutes at the beginning of the lesson looking at *Children of Britain Just Like Me* (*Ibid*, 1999). They talked about Sara Lee and her family's collection of Crown Derby. They downloaded information and pictures of Crown Derby from the Internet and looked at various photographs of the inside of trailers with Crown Derby on display. They also examined plates from across the world and produced their own designs inspired by the different styles and patterns. Some of the older Traveller children in the school gave a presentation about their parents' and grandparents' collections. Some of the parents sell china at car boot sales.

We have also used music lessons as a vehicle for raising all children's awareness of issues concerning Travellers. The team has produced *Moving On* (Cambridgeshire Multicultural Education Service, 2002), a CD of songs with linked lesson plans and team members have given interactive performances in schools. One school prepared the Year 3/4 pupils before the visit, tying the work in with literacy as well as music and producing a display for the school entrance. A team colleague who was involved in a *Skills for Life* project linked to media and the arts worked with a small group of Traveller adults and a theatre company to plan a demonstration of paper flower making. They also produced an explanatory leaflet and visited schools across the county to teach this skill to pupils. Another teacher in the team used *A Suitcase of History* containing items linked to traditional Traveller culture, together with photographs of fairgrounds dating back to the late nineteenth century, to work with a whole Year 3/4 class.

Evaluation, collation and moving on

All these initiatives were referenced in a *Literacy for All* conference where the county's director of education and HMI added weight to the evaluation and promotion of the work. The project gained further status and credibility when HMI visited three of the project schools and attended our final feedback meeting. Our work was quoted as an example of good practice in the *2001 National Literacy Strategy Annual Report* and information about the project appeared in the LEA's *Literacy Newsletter*, circulated to all schools, spreading the good work of the project to a wider audience.

Recently *Literacy for All* was relaunched to provide fresh impetus, create new, shared materials and see what progress had been made since we first started. This time, there are more participants. Many of those previously involved are again taking part, and we have managed to draw in new teachers and schools.

Feedback on the project is consistently positive. Formal feedback meetings enable partners to share their own enjoyment and that of their pupils with one another and LEA inspectors. This is where they excitedly describe the work they planned and the lessons they taught. High quality texts, focused planning, activities that drew on children's own experiences, opportunities for speaking and listening, and writing for a purpose were among the factors that have motivated pupils and teachers alike. Everyone agrees that partnership working at every level is making a real difference where it counts, in schools with individual classteachers and crucially with children of all minority and majority backgrounds.

I would like to acknowledge support from Bethan Rees (Advisory Teacher, Black and Bilingual Team), Karen Smith (Literacy Consultant) and my colleagues in the Team for Traveller Education, especially Joe Ferguson and Steve Redshaw.

10

Secondary Education –
Overcoming the Barriers

Sue Green and Louise Stokoe

Why do Traveller children underachieve so severely in the secondary phase? This chapter looks at the barriers that bar the path for older pupils. Case studies illustrate ways of overcoming those barriers, most notably by using school Self Review as a tool to aid inclusion.

> Every child has a fundamental right to education, and must be given the opportunity to achieve and and maintain an acceptable level of learning. (Salamanca Statement. UNESCO, 1994)

This chapter shares some of the experiences of secondary education of the Durham and Darlington Education Service for Travelling Children (DDESTC). We examine some of the barriers that impede the successful secondary education of Traveller children and explore ways in which they can be overcome.

Durham and Darlington Education Service for Travelling Children

The DDESTC is a consortium of two authorities. Durham is a large county and Darlington a small unitary authority. The majority of Travellers live on the five council authorised sites, the three council authorised sites leased to Gypsy wardens, a private site, a residential site, unofficial encampments and in houses. There are three small wintering sites in Durham for Fairground families. Circus families will seek school places or be educated in the mobile classroom. The Service has a Ford Transit mobile classroom which allows the authorities to offer education where there are practical difficulties for the children in accessing mainstream education. It also allows teachers to carry out initial assessment prior to school admission, particularly with large groups who are travelling together.

Secondary Traveller Education – the national overview

Raising the Attainment of Minority Ethnic Pupils (Ofsted, 1999) noted that no Traveller children had ever taken a GCSE exam in half the schools they surveyed and that many had opted out of the education system before the end of Key Stage 3. Ofsted concluded that 'raising the expectations of Gypsy Traveller pupils among secondary teachers is probably the most urgent priority'.

Studies of policies and practices that aim to improve the engagement of secondary aged Traveller pupils include Jordan, 1996, Kiddle, 1999, Lloyd *et al*, 1999 and several Ofsted documents. Most recent is *Aiming High: Raising the Achievement of Gypsy Traveller Pupils – A Guide to Good Practice* (DfES 2003). In 1996 Ofsted estimated there were 50,000 school aged Traveller children, while the Secretary of State for Education in 1997 thought the total number was significantly higher. Ofsted (1999) reported that Traveller pupils have the lowest exam results of any ethnic minority group.

The Ofsted report *Managing Support for the Attainment of Pupils from Ethnic Minority Groups* (2001) provides evidence of marked improvements nationally but reported that access, attendance and achievement are still a 'serious concern' and remain problematic in the secondary phase. Research carried out by Save the Children published in 2001 provided strong evidence that UK Travellers 'are being denied access to relevant education and mainstream schooling' and estimated that only 20 per cent of Traveller children of secondary age attended school. All this presents a serious picture of underachievement at secondary phase. What are the causes?

Secondary education and Travellers – the barriers

For some Travellers there is constant tension between maintaining their lifestyles and cultures and participating fully in public education and secondary school education presents a particular challenge. Travellers value financial independence, self-employment and the ability to operate successfully as a family unit. Secondary schools are seen as threatening to their cultural values and ethnic boundaries and arouse suspicion amongst many in the Traveller community. They believe that much of the curriculum is irrelevant to Traveller interests and lifestyles, and they could fear that prolonged schooling may erode a confident cultural and ethnic identity and weaken their physical resistance to the rigours of nomadic life. Their impressionable young people are seen to be vulnerable in secondary schools.

Many Traveller parents view secondary schools suspiciously as a threat to their strongly held moral values surrounding girl/boy relationships, formal and informal sex education, and drug use.

The transition to secondary school is also the time of transition into adulthood, when pupils should be learning skills that will support them as adults in the Traveller community. Some parents believe that it is enough that children have acquired basic educational skills during their primary years and that prolonged secondary schooling is an impediment to their maturity. The persistence and maintenance of their way of life depends heavily on avoiding experiences and influences that threaten to erode their value system. It is the community that can best prepare these young people for their adult roles within it.

These views create difficulties for young people who want to become involved in education and to experience new activities as this challenges cultural norms and can bring them into direct conflict with their families and their Traveller peers. Schools are social systems with rules. They can be pretty inflexible. And schools that are reluctant to adapt and differentiate the curriculum and school routines to meet the needs of Traveller pupils create barriers to the education of Travellers.

Research (Bhopal *et al*, 2001) has shown that promoting access and raising achievement for Traveller children depends greatly on the attitudes and actions of the schools in which the pupils are placed. Schools must fully embrace the concept of inclusion and recognise the need to continually monitor, review and revise policies and practice. An educationally inclusive school can be defined as one 'where teaching and learning, achievements, attitudes and the well being of every young person matter. Inclusive schools do not treat all young people the same but instead, take account of their varied life experiences and needs' (Ofsted, 2002a). Schools are now judged in the School Effectiveness section of the Ofsted report to determine if they are educationally inclusive.

The DfES has found that access, although improving, is still a significant difficulty 'especially for those children who are travelling from place to place and for the secondary age group in particular' (DfES, 2003). There is, for example, a conflict between the promotion of educational access, attendance and attainment of Traveller children and the Criminal Justice Bill, which requires local authorities to serve eviction notices on families camping on unofficial sites. Parents are reluctant to send children to school for fear of eviction. Children may be afraid that their home will no longer be there when they return from school so are reluctant to attend. Enforced movement disrupts education and deters attendance.

Barriers created by the education system

The education inclusion agenda is not helped by the demands imposed by school performance tables. For example, prolonged periods of non-attendance, despite being marked as an authorised absence when the family are travelling for the purpose of the family business, brings down school attendance figures. If there are large numbers of highly mobile pupils on a school's roll, this will affect the school's average attendance and can even trigger an Ofsted inspection.

For secondary aged pupils who travel through the spring or summer, continuous assessment procedures, particularly the building of portfolios for coursework in Year 10, cannot be managed. Key Stage 3 Standard Assessment Tests (SATs), selecting GCSE options at Year 9 and GCSE exams tend to clash with families' travelling patterns and prevent the young people being in school to take the exams. This also has an impact on performance tables.

Barriers created by the school

Not all schools provide culturally relevant resources. The school may have unrealistic homework expectations of children who return to families with low levels of literacy and to difficult home working conditions in a trailer.

Another barrier to access and achievement is the inflexibility of the curriculum and the reluctance of some schools to adapt and differentiate the curriculum and school routines. Staff, including front-line staff and non-teaching staff, are often unaware of the needs of Traveller pupils. Uniform and transport can both be barriers to continuing at school, since most sites are not within easy reach of public transport. Few LEAs exploit the flexibility they have in law to provide families with help with transport, despite current good practice guidance (Bhopal *et al*, 2000).

Overcoming the barriers – the inclusive school

There are however schools which strive to overcome such barriers facing Traveller children – schools that are characterised by a commitment to inclusivity. An example of one such in the DDESTC area is Riverside Comprehensive. Of its 841 pupils on roll, 283 (34 per cent) are on free school meals and there are 48 (17.5 per cent) Traveller pupils on roll. Provision for the education of pupils from the local Traveller community is a major strength of the school. The strong leadership and ethos of the school contributes significantly to the success of Traveller pupils in terms of confident relationships, improved access and academic achievement. The school demonstrates a strong commitment to the inclusion of Traveller pupils through its policies and actions. This commitment comes from the senior management team and the designated staff member for Travellers.

The designated teacher demonstrates through his actions that he sees it as a responsibility of the school to engage Travellers, to provide quality pastoral support and to work in partnership with parents. He has an excellent working knowledge of the Traveller community in the area and is well respected. Other senior members of staff have worked in partnership with the Traveller Education Service (TES) in developing relationships with parents, especially when difficulty arises. The school has shown a willingness to do outreach work with families, and this has helped to build trusting relationships. There is a spirit of mutual trust between the school and the Traveller community, as shown by the large number of parents who have chosen to send their children to Riverside.

Commitment to the inclusive ethos is critical to the success of the provision for Traveller pupils. The supportive and flexible arrangements and welcoming ethos of the school demonstrate its sensitivity to and supportiveness of the nomadic nature of some Traveller families. Riverside recognises that gaps in education can affect progress and that pupils may well need additional support. The school works in conjunction with TES staff to develop individual packages of support to help improve levels of achievement. The senior management team is happy to discuss and investigate alternative packages and they are currently funding twenty packages. This demonstrates a serious professional attempt to secure better participation rates and successful educational outcomes.

The professional development of school's staff with regard to Traveller issues is part of the generic programme of staff development. The key elements of good practice are evident in Riverside Comprehensive and are clearly having a positive effect on the education of *all* the pupils in the school.

Overcoming the barriers – the role of the Traveller Education Service

The development of TESs throughout the UK has been shown to improve Traveller children's access to educational provision and also to raise achievement. Her Majesty's Inspectorate of Schools (HMI, 1996) observed that inspections revealed that where schools had received significant support from TESs, the quality of learning and accuracy of knowledge for all pupils had improved. The DDESTC has a dedicated secondary team that provides opportunities for building relationships with families, schools and other agencies and establishing trust and mutual respect, working across authorities where appropriate.

TES work has been primarily driven by national directives attached to the main funding sources. Since April 2003, objectives have been driven by the Vulnerable Children Grant, 'to secure access to education, integration into school, regular school attendance, in school support and higher attainment' for Traveller children (DfES, 2003).

Historically, the focus of the delivery model to schools in many TESs has been primarily direct pupil/family focused activities. Services have also provided awareness-raising sessions for pupils and staff, developed and provided culturally specific resources, and developed independent learning materials for all children. The focus, however, has been on additional support for Traveller children who met service criteria and were thought to be at risk of underachievement.

Over the last two years key external drivers have necessitated a review of TES delivery models. This has caused a move towards a dual focus of direct pupil/family focused activities *and* an overt school improvement role.

Overcoming the barriers – schools' self review

One key initiative recently taken by the DDESTC to support school improvement and promote inclusion in light of these external drivers is the development of a self-review document *Monitoring and Evaluating Practice for Schools with Gypsies and Travellers on roll – a Self-Review for schools*. The purpose of the self review (SR) is threefold:

■ it enables any school to evaluate their educationally inclusive practice in respect of Traveller pupils and to form a hypothesis regarding their success

■ as Ofsted will now 'promote and draw from school self-evaluation' (Ofsted, 2003) it provides a mechanism for presenting Ofsted with evidence to test a school's hypothesis. 'The quality and use made of school evaluation is a good indicator of the calibre of management' (Ofsted, 2003).

■ it provides a tool for TESs to expand their school improvement role, through partnership working with schools to identify and support areas for development

Structure of the self review

The SR draws on four of the principal external drivers:

■ *Inspecting schools: Framework for inspecting schools* (Ofsted, 2003)

■ *Evaluating Educational Inclusion – Guidance for Inspectors and Schools* (Ofsted, 2002a)

■ *The Stephen Lawrence Inquiry* (Macpherson, 1999)

■ The Race Relations (Amendment) Act 2000

The SR is informed by the key elements of the Ofsted Evaluation Schedule and the key questions the inspectors must consider for all children. The SR is also linked to each of these key questions, so it offers the school additional questions to support the evaluation of educationally inclusive practice for Traveller pupils.

Existing Traveller outcomes

The SR starts, as does the Evaluation Schedule, with the outcomes for Traveller Pupils.

What progress have they made in your school? What is their attainment?

What accounts for the outcomes for Traveller pupils?

Having ascertained current outcomes, further questions follow:

What is the quality of other specified features?	How well are Gypsy and Traveller pupils' attitudes, values and other personal qualities developed?	How effective are teaching and learning for Gypsy and Traveller pupils?

What accounts for this?

How good is the quality of education in areas of learning, subjects and courses?	*What accounts for this?*	**What are the outcomes for Gypsy and Traveller pupils in your school?** **What is their attainment?** **How does this compare to other groups?**	*What accounts for this?*	How well does the curriculum meet Gypsy and Traveller pupils' needs?
How well is the school led and managed?		**What accounts for this?**		How well are Gypsy and Traveller pupils cared for, guided and supported?

How well does the school work in partnership with Gypsy and Traveller parents, other schools and the Gypsy and Traveller community?

The SR will add to a range of internal processes within school for specifically monitoring the levels of achievement and provision for Traveller pupils. It should feed into the School Improvement Plan, prioritising action and setting out programmes for implementation with support from the TES where appropriate. An example of the SR proforma is available at Appendix 3.

An example of self review in action

Senior staff at Riverside Comprehensive worked with TES staff to set up a self review working party, made up of a range of staff including a newly qualified teacher, to give a new perspective on the situation in their school. The TES teacher supported the school through the first stages of the SR then the working party continued with the review. It concluded that a top priority was to develop high quality independent and distance learning materials for use by all children who were out of school because of travelling, illness or exclusion as well as a small number of pregnant schoolgirls. The TES teacher worked with Heads of Department and subject teachers to develop independent learning materials based on the good practice model used by the TES to develop primary independent/distance learning materials in 1999. The SR enabled the school to identify its key Traveller pupil related needs.

Schools in both authorities in the DDTSC have welcomed the SR document, as it assists them to evaluate all the areas inspected by Ofsted and will help them to identify the possible challenges they face in seeking to be educationally inclusive. To use the SR document to its full potential, schools will need to be aware of the general issues regarding Traveller pupils – particulary equal opportunities and race relations legislation – and also take account of the situation, needs and attitudes of individual pupils. This requires training and awareness raising, which is provided by the DDTSC.

Support for self review – training

All schools in the DDTSC area with Traveller pupils on roll are offered in-service training. Information on the specific situations of Travellers is included within the context of equality issues and antiracist approaches. TES staff proactively encouraged schools to take up formal training. Schools in which training has taken place have benefited: teachers have actively sought to improve their practice by including information about Travellers in their teaching. For example the Holocaust is taught in the history curriculum. Gypsy music, art and designs include a trailer and a topic on town planning in geography includes a Gypsy site. An inclusive curriculum of this kind recognises diversity and demonstrates the schools' commitment to the principles of the Race Relations (Amendment) Act.

Some schools ask for support to write their Equal Opportunities Policy. One asked for help to review the impact of their homework policy on its ethnic minority pupils and another reviewed the policy on jewellery for all its pupils. The changes have come because the staff are having to challenge their own thinking and practice.

DDESTC have produced a reference pack that deals with a wide range of issues including history and culture, rights of the child and curriculum issues and this is distributed to all staff after training.

Flexing the curriculum

Inflexibility in the curriculum can be a barrier for Traveller children. A brief case study describes how Riverside Comprehensive overcame curriculum barriers, rethinking differentiation to meet the individual needs of each pupil.

Jake is in Year 11. He had hardly attended school in Year 10, preferring to go to work alongside his father in the family business. He viewed school as irrelevant to his needs and said he could learn more about earning his living by working with his dad. Jake is intelligent, has good literacy and numeracy skills and is computer literate. His mother was keen for him to attend school and joined the school as an adult learner to inform herself about education and enable her to help Jake with his schoolwork, whereas his father was happy for Jake to make his own choices. The Education Welfare Service was involved over his non-attendance but Jake still refused to attend school. A DDESTC team member visited the family at home and worked with them and the school to consider all possible options. No funding was available at the time for an alternative educational placement, so it was agreed that Jake return to school on a part time basis, integrated with work placement and work experience.

With the school, the family and the DDESTC team member working together, Jake was readmitted to school at the end of the autumn term. It was agreed that he was to come into school for two and half days a week to work towards GCSEs in English and Media Studies. His poor attendance in Year 10 meant he was behind with his coursework and needed support to catch up. So it was decided that Jake would work for half a day a week with the TES teacher, who would support him with his coursework, and would attend regular English and Media lessons on two days of the week. The rest of his week would be dedicated to work experience. This was to be formalised and a portfolio of evidence produced.

During the term Jake made excellent progress with his studies and produced some excellent coursework. It was clear that he would get a GCSE based on coursework only, but the grade he would receive would not reflect his true ability. Nonetheless, Jake did not want to sit the exam. The school staff thought Jake might be more likely to participate if he were allowed to sit his exam in a private room and not the exam hall and when this was suggested to Jake he agreed.

It transpired that part of the reason Jake did not wish to sit the exam was because he would be 'cooped up in a room with the windows and doors shut' which, for someone who spends so much time outdoors, was too much to bear. Interestingly, he always asked to sit near the window, preferable with it open, when he was in lessons. Jake was one of a few young people who found large classes difficult to cope with, so they were allowed outdoors for five minute breaks. This was identified as being important for certain pupils.

Jake had a good deal of positive feedback from school and DDESTC about the quality of his work and his positive attitude since he returned to school and this clearly contributed to his decision to stay. The teacher from DDESTC supported the school in their efforts to get special dispensation for Jake, telephoning the exam board and explaining the cultural significance of the request and writing the supporting statement. The exam board was accommodating and arrangements were duly made.

This is an example of a school taking account of one of its pupil's life experiences and needs and accommodating those needs with its flexible approach. The outcome was a young man with a positive experience of school and the education system who will be the first in his family to gain GCSE qualifications.

Alternatives to full-time school

Inadequate funding and resources can also be a barrier to education, for example when no funds are available for alternatives to mainstream education. Yet such alternative packages may be the way to ensure that certain young people can receive a continued, successful secondary education.

Rick, a Year 10 pupil, is a settled Traveller who attended school regularly until Year 9. During Year 10 his attendance began to decline, as he and his parents felt that he was at the age where school had few skills to offer that would be of use need to earn a living in his adult life.

The team helped Rick and his parents to complete an application to the LEA's Alternative Centre for Education (ACE) referral panel. The application was successful.

It was agreed that a vocational course would be most appropriate and Rick expressed particular interest in a building and bricklaying course.

Like all students who access alternative provision, he had to agree to continue also with literacy and numeracy studies.

Rick is now thoroughly enjoying his education and has not missed a single day at his alternative provision. What helped him to access such provision were: the rapid response to his declining school attendance, meaningful, positive discussion with all the people involved, and the willingness of the school to consider and ultimately fund an alternative placement.

A sanctuary area in school

Bhopal *et al* (DfEE, 2000) highlighted the need for 'sanctuary territory, a Traveller friendly space' to help give young Travellers the confidence to learn in a mainstream school.

The DDESTC bid through the Connexions service so they could provide a room for a designated workspace for the DDESTC teacher and as a Connexions access point. It was to be used as a place for Traveller children and their parents to meet with staff and access services, and also as a teaching room. The room was equipped with computers, printers, scanner, digital camera and a wide range of educational and cultural resources. The benefits have been enormous. Young people have a place to come, in small groups and individually, to be taught. Staff and parents can meet, and young people can easily access information from Traveller Internet sites, careers sites and Connexions. The ICT equipment has enabled Traveller pupils to make books about themselves and their families, inspired by *The Smiths* (NATT, 2002).

Some Year 7 and Year 8 pupils wrote an induction booklet for Year 6 pupils coming into the school, called *School's OK!* It featured photographs and text about the school and showed photographs of the authors and their friends enjoying school. The book showed that both the young people who produced it and those who were to receive it were being valued as members of the school community. *School's OK* was distributed on Traveller sites and a copy was given to every Traveller pupil who was to transfer to Riverside at the beginning of the next academic year. Now Traveller pupils are thinking about making a video, and about finding different ways of communicating with young people and their families.

Conclusion

We have schools in the two authorities that work hard to be inclusive and that are committed to meeting the needs of their young people. They provide flexible personal timetables, alternative curriculum, strong pastoral support, quality independent and distance learning materials and acknowledge preferred teaching and learning styles.

What these initiatives demonstrate is the commitment of secondary schools and the DDESTC to improve attendance and raise achievement of Traveller children in partnerships that enable collective responsibility.

The Government is pledged to raising standards of achievement for all children and to ensuring that all have access to the education system but there are still difficulties. General regulations and practices within the school and education system can create challenges to inclusion for *all* vulnerable children. The tension between education inclusion and school performance needs to be resolved. If school performance league tables are to remain, then the criteria that determine these rankings should include inclusivity. A framework against which Ofsted inspectors can judge the inclusiveness of a school is now available and should be used to promote educational inclusion. If schools can be awarded a position in a league table or a kite mark that publicly recognises and celebrates inclusivity, then all schools will be encouraged to work hard towards achieving equal opportunities and inclusiveness.

Ted Wragg (1999) has advanced the concept of changing and developing schools within a broader framework of 'sites of learning'. This offers a basis for debate about where, when and how young people can be educated. If the Government is committed to educational and social inclusion then this is the time for discussion about these issues and about the tensions between raising standards and inclusion.

11

Towards success in
secondary schooling

Barbara Blaney

Barbara Blaney has eighteen years experience as a Special Educational Needs Co-ordinator in a secondary school where Traveller pupils do well. Flexibility is the recurrent theme in this candid, in-depth account of how certain Traveller pupils succeed through Key Stages 3 and 4.

Mary's world

After all these years in Traveller Education I should have known better. But I had lost sight of how much we expect Traveller children to adapt. When we arrived at Mary's home I was struck by the culture gap between her home life and our school. We had been out for the day in the minibus with a number of students and dropped them all back home. Mary was the last. It was a sunny day in June and as fifteen year old Mary, immaculate in her school blazer and tie, got out, her younger siblings ran past chickens and dogs to greet her. Mary's parents followed and her grandfather looked up to wave from the cart he was mending. The horses were stabled and the whole family was outdoors. It looked like a homestead in a western film.

The family waved as I left and I thought 'What hoops are we putting these young people through?' We insist on uniforms, homework, pens, but this is a different world.

Our world – Chalvedon secondary school

At our school of 1800 pupils in Basildon, Essex, we usually have between ten and fifteen Travellers on roll. The Travellers might be housed, live on a twenty four plot council Traveller site two miles away or on private sites, and occasionally we have roadside Travellers and children from Showman families. The school has a long history of welcoming Travellers and this is reflected around the school. We have worked consistently and successfully to counter and eradicate the racism, prejudice and hostility too often directed at Travellers.

Flexibility is a key approach

> I come to school even though I don't always want to. I wouldn't have come but my granny and mum said I should. They said I should be able to read and write, as they know it is difficult if you can't do these things. *Sarah*

The active involvement and support of headteacher Alan Roach has been crucial in our effective provision for Travellers. He takes the line:

> We never knowingly compromise our policies but we can and do adopt a flexible approach to school rules and procedures. This is the key to our sensitive provision for Travellers.

Flexibility in attendance, timetables and chaperones

Attendance and punctuality can be problems for schools but the flexible approach referenced above can be illustrated by Susie's situation.

Although Susie and her family lived in a house two miles from school, each month and most weekends, she visited one of her married sisters on sites in Essex and Cambridgeshire. Her attendance had always been poor but on her return, her form teacher and her peers always welcomed her. Members of her form and her teaching groups did not question Susie's lack of homework or proper equipment but were always willing to help Susie in her work.

The family had no clocks, so Susie arrived when she was ready. On arrival at school, she called into Pupil Services (the school's department which I supervise) or found her form teacher to find out what lesson she should be in. The school has a strict policy about punctuality but flexibility in the rules meant that Susie was never reprimanded for lateness. She knew that if she had a problem about uniform it would be sorted out.

For Danielle, offering the option of a flexible timetable was the key to persuading her to come to school. Her mother and younger sister had come to look round the school. As we were completing the necessary forms, I asked whether there were other members in the family who might like to come to school. The hesitation in replying suggested that this was the case. Understanding that there would be no pressure on her, fourteen year old Danielle came to visit the school. She had had no schooling since aged ten, had a low level of literacy and was worried about her ability to cope with school. She felt at home right away and began by attending only some lessons. Before long she wanted to go to all of them. After only three weeks in school she took part in an English speaking and listening assignment, where she abandoned the notes she had made and spoke from the heart about Travellers. Her eloquence and passion held the class spellbound. Danielle stayed with us for six months before moving on.

> I could stand up in my English class because I had confidence in myself and that other pupils would not laugh at me. In other schools if I did that they would laugh at me and call me a gyppo... *Danielle*

The school is popular and there is always a waiting list for places. Esther wanted to go on roll but there was no place for her in Year 7. Instead, she attended in uniform once a week for an hour, working in the Learning Support Base until a place became available. In the meantime, her subject teachers provided her with books, so that when she officially started she had already completed some of the work. This was one illustration of part-time timetabling that ultimately led to full time, successful attendance.

For pupils new to education, attending part time may be the best option until they feel more secure. If an hour a day is all a pupil can manage at first, that is what will be arranged. Rose aged 14, came from a Showman's family and had experienced unhappy times at her previous, winter school. The Traveller Education Service (TES) asked what we could offer. Rose was worried about being in school but we arranged for her to come in with her mum for two hours, twice a week to work in the Learning Support base. At first Rose did not want her mother to leave but gradually her confidence grew until she was able to stay on her own for several hours. Teachers came in to see her and discuss the work she had been doing for them. Rose never managed to go into a classroom but was able to work in the library on a computer alongside other students. It was the freedom to work flexibly that offered a chance of education to Rose. Any insistence that she attend full time or had to go into class would have been fruitless. She moved on after a few months and we lost track of her.

One Year 7 pupil attended lessons for her first three weeks accompanied by her seventeen year old aunt who had left school the previous year. Another Year 7 pupil was persuaded to go into lessons when a Year 9 Traveller at the school whom he knew agreed to go with him. Sometimes siblings can be put together in the same class. Currently we have Year 10 Rachel and Year 8 Leah together in the same Year 8 class. Rachel had previously dropped out after one term in Year 7 but decided to return when she found she could attend with her sister. When arrangements such as these are announced in staff briefings they are accepted without question.

Joe and Dan, roadside Travellers who were stopping in a lay-by a few miles away, were challenging. We accommodated them by similar flexible methods. They had never attended school but had joined a local boxing club and wanted to fight in the Schoolboy Boxing Championship. They arrived one morning with their boxing coach, declaring that they wanted to come to school. We decided that they should both go into the same Year 7 class even though Joe was 14. They attended morning sessions, going to some lessons with support and spending the rest of the time learning to read and write. Although they were only with us for a month, they achieved some real progress. As we waited in the car park one day, Dan was recounting what he had learned that day. He acted out the earth revolving round the sun then exclaimed, 'Isn't it wonderful, how every morning the sun comes up and every evening it goes down again. That's wonderful that is!'

Flexibility about the curriculum

If a particular curriculum area causes concerns for a pupil, our approach is, 'Let's not worry about Drama for now, come and do some extra reading instead.' Physical Education (PE) is often a problem but if having PE on their timetable means pupils will not attend school, we accept that it is better for them to attend school and not do PE.

Rachel and Leah did not go to Drama lessons for six weeks. Then it became clear that they thought that Drama meant acting on a stage. After we had explained what was actually involved and they were offered the chance to go with a teaching assistant to watch, they were quite willing to attend. The teacher was alerted that they were coming and told that she should not expect them to participate. Within two weeks both girls were actively taking part in drama lessons. But neither girl will take part in class PE lessons – although they do put on trainers and go out with a teaching assistant to play badminton and basketball. If the school had insisted that all lessons must be attended, the girls would have quit.

Flexibility in administration and policy

We do not insist upon absence notes where we know parents are illiterate. First day phone calls are only made to Traveller homes once absence has been checked with a teacher from the TES. We appreciate the many reasons for absence: time off when a new baby is born, regular long weekends away to take part in harness racing or visits to fairs.

Although our uniform policy forbids hooped earrings, we make exceptions for Travellers, treating them as symbols of their culture so we give the heads of year groups a list of Traveller pupils. Other pupils have no difficulty accepting the special allowance for Travellers.

Support for teachers

As part of their induction, all new teachers at Chalvedon are given a copy of a booklet compiled and produced by the school, *My Mother Said*. This highlights the importance of our commitment to Travellers, tries to provide basic information about Traveller culture and identity and includes exercises for the teachers to complete. The response to this booklet is always positive. New teachers have told me that they read it from cover to cover and that they found it the most useful text in their induction literature.

Some Traveller pupils are registered as having special needs, so have an Individual Education Plan (IEP). As part of the IEP, teachers are informed that the pupil is from a Traveller background. One girl's IEP, for example, begins: 'Sarah is from a traditional Traveller family and is keen to learn though she has literacy difficulties'. The IEP also explains if pupils are out of their chronological year group and offers advice to teachers. Sarah's includes:

- welcome Sarah to your lessons

■ do not comment on lack of homework

■ provide any missing equipment

Teachers find it useful to have a base to which Travellers and other pupils can resort. One able Traveller boy, Tom in Year 8, arrives if he is having a difficulty in a lesson. The problem is usually with a supply teacher who has not appreciated the fact that Traveller boys, like most adolescents, respond best when they are spoken to as adults. He happily does his work in the Learning Support Base, with or without help.

Other support for the school comes from links with the TES. This is valuable, especially in connecting with children in primary school. We aim to fit in extra visits for Traveller pupils in Year 6 so that they feel comfortable with the transition from primary to secondary school. So for example, the TES and the school jointly planned a lunch at school for parents of Year 6 Traveller children. Three families took up the offer, creating an additional opportunity to make contact and complete the application forms.

Beyond Key Stage 3

Keeping pupils long enough to take GCSEs is not easy, so we are ready to make concessions to enable them to complete whatever courses they can. If this means part time schooling then we will arrange it. There is sometimes family resistance to pupils continuing in education beyond the age of thirteen. It can be difficult for boys in particular to be still at school at fifteen or sixteen as their fathers may feel they should be out earning a living.

Stanley attended school one day a week during Years 10 and 11 and managed to complete work for GCSE English and Maths. He spent the other four days working with his father. Now the treasurer of a local Gypsy church, he reminded me when we met recently of the time we spent on his maths and remarked, with a grin, how useful it had turned out to be.

Bill had had enough of school by the end of Year 10 and wanted to go and work with his uncle. We examined his timetable and decided that he could pass GCSE Science and GCSE Maths. So that he could complete coursework or catch up on science practicals, we arranged that he would come into school whenever I asked him to. He came whenever I telephoned and the science and maths teachers gave him however much time he needed. By March of Year 11 all his coursework was complete. He was given the exam dates and promised to attend. I lost touch with him and worried lest he would forget so I telephoned his home and was told he was working in Europe. On the day of the first exam he turned up, saying: 'I told you I wouldn't let you down! All I need is a pen, pencil and calculator and I'll be all right'.

Bill now has three GCSEs at Grade E.

Realising potential – the inclusive goal

At fifteen, Ellen found herself the only young person in her extended family who was still attending school and was often mocked for this by her cousins, aunts, and uncles. Fortunately her mother valued education and encouraged Ellen to continue at school for as long as she wanted. Ellen's mother was herself criticised for her attitude by men in the family, who warned their wives to keep away from her influence and ideas about education.

After an extended time of travelling Ellen fell behind with her coursework and was ready to give up. We planned that she should drop three subjects and concentrate on the rest. She did so for a month but gradually picked up all the subjects again and took ten GCSEs/GNVQs, achieving five higher grades. Ellen is now taking an arts foundation course.

Her mother has maintained her support for education, telling female relations that Ellen now has the choice of a career or settling down with a family. She recently recounted how a number of family members originally hostile to this idea had told her that her decision was a good one. On the day she left Ellen wrote the school a letter:

> This letter comes from the heart ... I want you to be pleased that you have influenced a Traveller child ... and made them realise that there is something in life rather than cleaning and cooking, but making something of yourself. *Ellen*

Stanley, Ellen, and Bill are just three of the pupils who would have left school with no formal qualifications if we had not been prepared to be flexible.

Traveller culture/school culture

We encourage Traveller pupils to be proud of their culture.

> I want people to know what we're like and tell people that we're not all wild and that all people are different. *Danielle*

We make explicit statements of acceptance and welcome to the Traveller community. The main school corridor has three display boards which celebrate Traveller culture, including photos and postcards brought back from Appleby Fair by pupils, explanations of fairground rides and the work of the Showman's Guild, and other pieces of work by pupils. We celebrated our links with the local Traveller community as part of our Charter Mark Award and this too is clearly acknowledged in the reception area.

We encourage Traveller pupils to respond to portrayals of Travellers in the media, whether negative and stereotypical or positive.

Over the years there has been correspondence between the editor of *The Sunday Times* colour supplement and two Traveller pupils, and letters to local papers about reports, including one to congratulate a reporter on her positive portrayal of Travellers. A pupil wrote a letter to the writer and producer of *The Bill.* A pupil at a private school who wrote a poem, *Gypsy,* published in the school's magazine and its headteacher also received letters. Louise wrote to correct the young poet's misconceptions about Travellers, explaining that she was not in the habit of walking 'barefoot among the daisies' and did not have rotten teeth.

We believe that these small responses help Traveller pupils to see that their culture is worth defending, and we empower them to do something about it.

The involvement of the school with Traveller families goes beyond the classroom. The school belongs to the Gypsy Council. We are available to sign passport forms and help in obtaining birth certificates. I have had conversations with registrars in the Republic of Ireland and the UK to help identify birth certificates for adults who are unsure of their exact date and place of birth or their full name. One woman was delighted to find that she was a year younger than she had thought!

> Travellers have a very strict rule of cleanliness. Clothes are never washed in the same bowl as dishes because that is dirty. Tea towels are washed separately from all the other washing because to mix them would be dirty. *Lisa*

Teachers try to take account of Traveller culture within the curriculum. In art, pupils are asked to draw a sketch of a room in their home, not their house. History and Religious Education acknowledge the often forgotten Gypsy Holocaust and coursework for GCSEs in various subjects has included work on Appleby Fair, looking after a child in a trailer and how to groom horses. As part of Year 10 GNVQ art, a unit on the fairground was included and a parent came in to talk to the group, bringing with her photographs, journals and books to illustrate the art of the fairground. The food technology classrooms now have sinks labelled 'Hand washing only' as teachers have responded to Traveller *mokkadi* rules. These culturally determined rules dictate that Travellers do not wash cutlery and crockery in the same bowl as one in which hands have been washed. The subject teacher also takes care to tell all pupils that the washing machine and tumble drier are only ever used for tea towels and dishcloths.

Travellers succeed – school succeeds

> I have never been called names here because I think most people respect us, maybe because Chalvedon has had Travellers a lot. The teachers all help me and don't make a thing about that I can't read much... Pupils always help me to write things down and the teachers never mind. *Danielle*

The presence in school of Traveller pupils makes a tremendous contribution to the learning experience of the other pupils and adults in the institution and some prevailing prejudices are challenged. Should some of the *gaujos* (non-Travellers) educated alongside Travellers one day become councillors or MPs, they might make informed decisions about Traveller issues.

The concluding paragraph of the headteacher's foreword to *My Mother Said* sums up the value to our school of Travellers:

> It is very evident that the school benefits from the presence of our Travellers. For example their morality and cleanliness have caused many non-Travellers to question their own prejudices; their family loyalty and respect for their parents and extended family are an example to their non-Traveller peers; they provide cultural diversity in an otherwise homogenous community. Furthermore the learning support and pastoral care of Travellers at Chalvedon has helped our teachers to appreciate that all pupils are individuals with needs. Our Travellers have been integrated into the school without compromise to their identity; as a result the school has gained.

12

Keys to success: individual Traveller pupils' secondary experiences

The Buckinghamshire METAS team

The Buckinghamshire METAS team illustrate how two Traveller pupils, Paddy and Sarah, have succeeded at secondary school. These case studies offer clues to what promotes success for secondary Traveller pupils.

Introduction

This chapter focuses on the experiences of two Year 7 Traveller pupils during their first year of secondary education and shows how the school and the Minority Ethnic and Traveller Achievement Service (METAS) worked together to support them. Every child is an individual and the issues and situations described here pertain to these two children but we hope the case studies will help those who work with Traveller pupils in secondary school to raise their achievement.

Secondary transfer – Sarah and Paddy

Two Traveller children joined Chesham Park Community College in the south of Buckinghamshire in Year 7. They came from different backgrounds. Sarah is a housed Traveller living in the catchment area. She had received targeted support in Year 6 to ensure good SATs results and to support the family through transfer. Sarah had had difficulties accessing the curriculum and this affected her behaviour in the classroom. Much time was given to supporting her and her parents in managing the primary school Pastoral Support Plan.

Given her primary school report, staff at her new school were concerned whether they could meet Sarah's needs. However, she already
had a sister in the school. METAS worked to empower Sarah's new
teachers by discussing her needs with the head of year and the special
educational needs co-ordinator (Senco). It was decided that Sarah's
Traveller liaison worker should support her during the first term of
secondary school. A meeting was arranged in the second week of term
to decide criteria for support and discuss the settling in period. Crucial
information was exchanged about Sarah's views and the potential flash-
points to be avoided. Timetabled support was given in critical lessons
until the school felt familiar enough with Sarah's needs to manage the
relationship effectively on their own.

Paddy was from the north of the county and living on a private site
awaiting planning permission. As all the secondary schools near his site
were full, he was placed in Chesham Park, and transport was provided
via a taxi shared with other non-Traveller children.

An initial meeting was held between Paddy, his parents, school and the
support teacher, who had established a relationship with the family
during their first year of settled schooling. For Traveller parents with
little or only negative experience themselves of formal education, this
meeting was crucial. His mother was warmly received by the head of
year, given a brief talk about the school, its ethos and aims and then encouraged to ask questions. The staff raised some matters the family
hadn't asked about, like sports kit. Uniform was not a problem. The
head of year had her own questions abut Paddy's likes and learning.
Smiles confirmed that a good first impression was made on both sides.
The school's responsibility and concern for their child was evident to
the parents. The family was taken on a tour of the school and staff took
time to say hello.

Finding their feet – transition strategies

The school operates a unit called the Middle Room, run by an experienced member of staff. The unit is for any students who are finding
integration into full time school difficult. One room is set aside for
students to work one-to-one with the head of the unit at times during
the day so they can talk to her and develop strategies for coping. As she
says: 'I am paid to have the time to bring children in from the cold'. A
meeting with the head of year and the Senco established that Paddy
would benefit from working in the Middle Room during the autumn

term and his timetable included some periods working one-to-one within the unit. Paddy knew if things got too much for him during the day he could always visit the unit. The support teacher made regular visits during this first term to offer pastoral and in-class support alongside home-school liaison.

During the first term there were occasional incidents in which Paddy found himself in trouble for fighting, mostly because of provocation or misunderstandings. The Middle Room swung into action without fail, providing counselling and strategies for temper management and, most importantly, an understanding personal touch. He was listened to and made aware that he was not going to be blamed out of hand for throwing a punch but that he was not justified in resolving disagreements with his fists. He did find himself on internal exclusion once or twice and understood that he had done wrong. His form tutor telephoned his mother weekly to let her know what sort of week he had had and both school and the METAS maintained close home-school links.

Keys to success – tackling racism and training
Early in the first term a vital whole school inset covering aspects of Traveller culture was provided by the METAS. This fell during the school's Ofsted inspection and was attended by all the staff and provided an opportunity for frank and open exchanges of views, giving the staff a better appreciation and awareness of their Traveller pupils' lifestyle. Following this, meetings took place with subject teachers to discuss specific learning needs and suggest strategies for teaching. Staff were keen to learn about Paddy's previous school experience, which sadly was very limited.

The school's willingness to respond to the needs of the Traveller children was immediate. When Sarah felt that she had been the target of racist behaviour and was suspended for reacting physically, the headteacher met with her parents and the head of year to deal with the incident.

The school behaviour policy was clear – there was zero tolerance of racism of any kind. All incidents were dealt with in line with county guidelines (Bucks. County Council, 2002) issued to every school. The METAS advised the school how to relate equality issues to the curriculum and a county trainer was brought in to work with the entire year group on antiracism. Headteachers generally set the tone for their school and its ethos. This headteacher led by example, knowing all the pupils' names and taking an active interest in everything they did – an example followed by the staff.

Teachers established excellent relationships with the Traveller pupils, treating them firmly but fairly; showing that they cared about them and treating them as individuals but within the school rules. Staff were in regular contact with home via weekly phone calls and meetings with METAS staff. These meetings enhanced the understanding of Traveller culture and also the families' appreciation of what this caring school was trying to achieve for their children.

Keys to success – an active sense of belonging
Traveller children often find it hard to see themselves as part of the school's larger body. The school tried to overcome this sense of isolation. Paddy enjoyed all physical contact sports and when he learnt that the school needed players for a Year 7 rugby team he went along to the trials. He was thrilled to be selected for the side and when the school played its first match at home his father came to watch, shouting encouragement from the touchline. Staff were delighted that his father had come along, as it showed a real commitment to the school and was a great step forward. This active involvement from a Traveller father in his child's school and education was a measure of the success being achieved.

Towards the end of the autumn term it was time for Paddy to go into lessons full time. As part of leaving Middle Room he received an award at a presentation ceremony in front of invited guests, including his parents. Along with his certificate, he received a gift of a fountain pen and a Christmas card from the Middle Room staff. What was especially pleasing was the fact that he could read his parents the message in the card.

Keys to success – raising self-esteem
As part of Paddy's history coursework he had to construct a timeline. After several weeks and visits to the Internet and the school library, his timeline took shape: a strip of paper, left to right, with the dates from 0 to 1991, properly placed, three word-processed labels, 'Jesus', 'Hastings' and at the end, 'Paddy'. This enchanted him. Lack of self-esteem can be a major problem for Traveller children, especially in secondary schools. They often find themselves behind in basic literacy and feel there is little recognition of their family's way of life, history or values.

Working on his timeline project, Paddy was able to achieve excellent coursework, build relationships with several staff and find expression for his own culture. He included John Cunningham in his project, a Traveller from Yorkshire who won the Victoria Cross in the First World War. In planning discussions he happened to mention his great uncle who played the Irish Eulean pipes and was a legend in Ireland during the 1930s. Much to Paddy's delight, the support teacher managed to find one of his great uncle's recordings called *The Bunch of Keys*. Searching the Internet produced more information about the great piper and Paddy's eyes were out on stalks! He gave his great uncle Johnny pride of place on the timeline, along with Henry VIII and William the Conqueror.

This timeline project was typical of how Paddy was helped to feel he was included within the school – his own culture standing there alongside great events in British history. Before that September, he had completed about two years of education in his life.

As Paddy thrived, so too did Sarah. As she and her parents became more familiar with school they established comfortable working relationships with the staff, and so the work of the METAS became less hands-on and intensive and the school was able to play its full part in her education. Support from the METAS was reduced to a monitoring role.

Tragedy and the close knit family

In the weeks just before Christmas, Paddy's cousin died tragically in a caravan fire – surprisingly, still not uncommon. During the following weeks, METAS support was available for him on a daily basis. The Middle Room provided counselling sessions for him and told him if he needed to withdraw at any time during the day from lessons and talk about his feelings, he could. The head of year made the entire staff aware of the tragic accident and asked for their understanding, and staff made every effort to help him through this sad time. They listened when he spoke and the school provided a place of stability for him where smiles were the order of the day. Paddy was valued and life went on.

The future

Building on past positive educational experiences and responding actively to on-going issues and even tragedies, the school can now plan for future success. Further development of differentiated work is a priority. During the summer term departments will be asked to produce outlines of what they intend to cover in Year 8 and staff from the Special Needs team will differentiate these lessons, producing materials to improve access for students with limited reading skills. METAS will input resources to reflect Traveller culture.

Resources will be further supplemented. For example, the school has bought, and already made good use of, *The Smiths* reading scheme (NATT, 2002) and hopes to use other materials for recording information in each lesson.

Most upsets and problems with behaviour have stemmed from a pupil's limited experience of operating in a school environment and understanding the rules, but there is also frustration when pupils are unable to record information. This in part is due to unrealistic expectations of what a student who has had a severely interrupted schooling can do. Here lies the crux of the issues relating to Traveller secondary pupils' underachievement.

Another recurring issue for Traveller pupils is record transfer, which applies even within school. In Chesham Park Community College all Year 8 teachers will receive a student profile, outlining strategies after they have consulted the Traveller pupils themselves, and this will be used to support the pupils' future learning.

Mobility or extended absence is another recurring issue. For example, Sarah was reluctant to return to school after one holiday. The METAS worker and the head of the inclusion unit met to arrange for her to go to Middle Room before registration if she felt uncomfortable facing her classmates after a long absence. The head of the unit visited the family at home to talk things through. Providing this gentle way of returning to school solved the problem. Future issues will be addressed with equal sensitivity.

Conclusion

Achieving positive outcomes with these two secondary aged Traveller pupils involved both reactive and proactive responses. Yet it is clear that throughout, those responses were couched within a supportive whole school policy, management and teaching and learning style. It appears that to address Traveller pupil underachievement at secondary school, a combination is needed of micro individual, teacher level responses and macro whole school responses. Used together, they can shape the keys for success and unlock the potential educational achievement of all Traveller pupils.

13

Developments in supported distance learning

Ken Marks

Tracing the history of Distance Learning support for travelling pupils, Ken Marks applies a theoretical learning triangle model to identify good practice and enable assessment of new forms of electronic learning at a distance.

This chapter looks at developments and good practice in the use of distance learning for school age children in Traveller communities. It draws on initiatives, particularly from the 1990s, to highlight an ideal model of practice which has the base school at its heart and an integral supportive role for Traveller Education Services (TESs). It also looks to a future where Information Communication Technology (ICT) will increasingly have the potential to narrow the gap between teacher and distance learner and raises some questions about the roles of schools and TESs, particularly at secondary level.

The context: A mobile lifestyle

Supported distance learning evolved as a response to the mobile lifestyles of many Traveller families. However, any attempt to home in on Traveller mobility has to acknowledge that the travel patterns of the different Gypsy communities, of the Fairground and Circus families and of New Travellers all vary enormously. They vary across the year. They vary in duration. They vary from local/regional to national and even international. They also vary in purpose, from, for example, the celebration of cultural events to economic activity. For some, like the Fair-ground and Circus communities, mobility means a series of more or less planned moves over the working season. At the other extreme there are still something of the order of 3,000 Gypsy families forced to live an unpredictable roadside existence (Kenrick and Clarke, 1999).

Consequently distance learning evolved as part of a range of TES responses to mobility, which, for example, continue to embrace outreach responses (mobile units and peripatetic staff who visit sites) and improved shared-information initiatives intended to ease discontinuity as pupils move from school to school whilst travelling. It is not *the* solution to mobility, but rather an approach which can come into its own where families have a secure base for part of the year and where mobility is relatively high in terms of moving from place to place or there are other reasons why children are unlikely to gain a positive experience from trying to link in with local schools as they travel.

Supported distance learning: evolving practice

As noted by Pat Holmes and her co-authors, even where schools give good support when children are attending, they can easily fail to extend this level of service to cover periods of travel. 'Children have been sent away with a pile of textbooks and materials designed for guided class-room use rather than independent study' (Holmes *et al*, 2000). From their inception many TESs began to make links with such base schools, to encourage thinking about support whilst children were away, and, where appropriate, to play a part in designing and developing more suitable learning packs. Anecdotal evidence suggests that this activity was often centred on Fairground pupils, probably for two inter-related reasons. Showchildren may travel for nine or even ten months of the year, and can be moving from place to place on a weekly basis. Such a pattern was clearly problematic for school attendance and some new form of provision was needed to balance discontinuities. Nonetheless, the 5,000 or so families which make up the UK Fairground community returned regularly to their own local yards during the winter period and had a community expectation that children, at least at primary level, would return to their local base schools. TESs were therefore able to build up working relationships with these schools, and perhaps more importantly with the parents, during the winter season. This pattern offered a relatively secure platform for the development of distance education, and indeed such moves have been supported by the ten

Children using traditional, paper-based packs.

regional Sections that make up the Showmen's Guild (the major national organisation representing the Fairground community). This Fairground focus was not exclusive, but seems to have played a major part in early initiatives.

As TESs gained and shared experience, it is possible to trace some interesting and valuable markers that point the way towards good practice and to the future. It seems useful to present these within a framework drawn from the broader literature of distance education, but which also highlights the nature of the challenge and the potential future role of ICT. The framework is illustrated in Figure 1 on page 110 and is adapted from a model first outlined by Amundsen (1993)

Amundsen's triangle was intended to highlight the three components of the classic teaching/learning situation: the teacher, the learner and the learning content or programme. She associates these components with the apexes of a triangle, and uses the sides to illustrate the way in which interactions should surround and support a planned learning process. Adapted as a descriptive tool, this diagram is useful in contrasting the

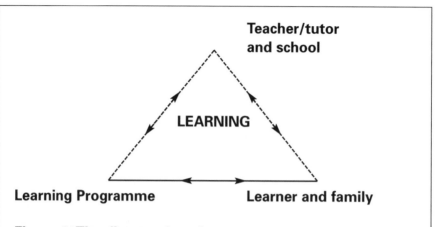

Figure 1: The distance learning process
(The dotted sides of the triangle illustrate the challenge of weakened interactions)

face-to-face classroom environment with the distance learning context. In the traditional (pre-Internet) mode of distance learning key aspects of interactivity are radically constrained. The learner's direct inter-actions often relate almost entirely to the tasks they pursue within their packs. Interactions with the teacher can be infrequent and certainly lack immediacy. Equally the teacher's scope to adapt materials in the light of evidence of pupil progress is delayed and often limited. These points are illustrated in the figure by the use of dotted lines for the weakened interactions.

The diagram is also useful as a visual representation of what Moore has called the challenge of 'transactional distance'. Moore (1991) set out to draw attention to the psychological and communication space between learner and distant teacher rather than the more obvious physical/time separation. This was a space of potential misunderstandings and learn-ing blockages, which could lead to feelings of isolation and frustration and consequent loss of motivation. However, Moore suggested that there were two factors that could reduce such distance. One was increased dialogue between teacher and learner, that is, a strengthen-ing of one side of the triangle. The other was the 'responsiveness' of the programme to learner needs, and here again a strengthening of one side of the triangle has a critical part to play. Moore also suggested that the impact of transactional distance would relate directly to the degree of independent learning skills which individual learners had developed.

Having introduced a framework within which to describe emerging good practice, this can now be described in three sections that correspond to the apexes of the triangle: the learner, the pack and the teacher. The material used is mainly drawn from the results of projects funded via the European Federation for the Education of Occupational Travellers (EFECOT). They reflect an approach that emphasises the importance of the base school, supported by the TES, as at the heart of the process and do not claim to give a comprehensive overview. But when one looks at themes shared at workshops and conferences coordinated by the National Association of Teachers of Travellers (NATT), the materials do seem to reflect what was being learned from a broader burst of activity and experimentation that started in the early 1990s and gained momentum throughout the decade.

Although the focus is therefore on traditional (pre-Internet) practice there is also a brief overview of developments that relate directly to the use of ICT to strengthen the distance learning experience.

The learner, the family and the community context

> We got involved in making this magazine because we have had experience of working on our own. We know what it is like to have no help around when you get stuck and you need it. Some of our mothers give us a lot of encouragement, some don't. Some teachers help more than others. Mostly we had to do it on our own and cope the best way we could. (Devon Traveller Education Service, 1998)

This is the introductory paragraph of a magazine, *Get it Sorted*, produced by a group of Fairground children who were asked to comment on their experiences of distance learning over a period of years. Taken together with its sequel, *Fair comment: Parents' views of Distance Learning* (Devon Consortium Traveller Education Service, 1999) this publication gives a fascinating insight into how it feels to be at the learner/family apex of Amundsen's triangle.

The magazines illustrate what TESs were discovering about the lifestyles of Traveller communities and the practical difficulties of doing schoolwork in a family trailer environment. The contributions draw attention to the many distractions of a travelling lifestyle and the need for children to 'learn the business' as well as working with the school pack. They highlight tensions about the value of schoolwork, particularly at secondary level, variable commitment from both children and parents, and, sadly, variable commitment and quality of support from some schools.

This is no rosy picture; the contributors tell it as it is and set a realistic context to the challenge faced by TESs and base schools. However, both children and parents also share good and bad experiences, and point the way to important aspects of good practice. Comments about learning packs resonate strongly with recommendations from other TES documentation (see below) and, referring back to the diagram, highlight the critical importance of working (interacting) with well designed and relevant distance learning materials.

The comments also highlight the importance of learner-tutor communication; from the learner perspective the other critical side of the triangle. If there were misunderstandings and learning blocks, the common response seems to have been to give up on the unit of work until a teacher visited or it was possible to go into school. However, there were also good examples of families who had been encouraged by staff and who picked up the phone, or used fax, to contact either the base-school or the TES.

The magazines offer a valuable resource, particularly because of their strong 'how does it feel' perspective. However, it is also useful to draw on the earlier EFECOT publication *What is your school doing for travelling children: a guide to equal opportunities through distance learning* (EFECOT, 1994). This publication was produced with support from the West Midlands Consortium Education Service for Travelling Children (WMCESTC), but clearly reflects similar messages from other TESs.

In terms of the learner/family apex, the document stresses that teachers need to start with awareness. They need to be aware of cultural strengths and values of Traveller communities, including their oral traditions and practical, problem solving, orientation. They need an understanding of related mobility patterns and the implications for exchanging work. They need to take account of the busy home/trailer environment and to decide how much schoolwork is appropriate and realistic (something between 6-10 hours emerges in the unpublished literature as an informal rule of thumb).

This awareness perspective is complemented by a focus on the need to celebrate and strengthen the skills of parents as partners. Indeed this perspective comes across even more strongly in other unpublished documentation. Theirs is a crucial role in encouraging and, wherever possible, supporting learning in the trailer home. They need to be prepared for this role. However, many parents had negative experiences of schooling, lack the confidence to work with teachers or to support their children's efforts, and can be embarrassed by their own poor literacy. Best practice from TESs includes examples of work over time which has led to parents sharing their wealth of experience, becoming involved in the classroom, and becoming fully involved with planning for distance learning support. It also includes a formal training initiative, *Parents as Educators*, within the north west region (Kenyon and Shannon, 2000) which, for all its early problems, remains an important marker for the future.

The learning pack

The learning pack is at the heart of traditional distance learning. As an apex of the learning triangle, it is the immediate focus for the learner. It is not just about learning activity but needs to lead, guide, motivate and wherever possible give internal feedback. One seminal work on design, written by Derek Rowntree, suggests that the challenge is to create a 'teacher-in-a-package' (Rowntree, 1992). In the Traveller context, the EFECOT overview publication gives a useful set of pointers which again reflect other unpublished material produced by TESs (*op cit*, 1994). These start with an emphasis on the importance of taking coordinated decisions within the base school, for example prioritising curriculum coverage, and move on to consider aspects of format, design and type of pack content.

This discussion is effectively summarised in a series of pointers for success (here reordered and slightly reworded to draw in pointers from other sections of the document):

Learning material and related activities

■ Work needs to be broken down into manageable units, and the quantity of work needs to reflect both the families' working practices and a realistic assessment of what the children may be expected to achieve on their own

■ Units of work need to be of manageable length, and should be designed with clear learning objectives

■ Materials need to be at an appropriate level for individual students and designed for working in the home environment rather than with classroom support

■ Materials should be stimulating and make use of appropriate media (audio and video as well as text)

■ Wherever possible, they also need to enable learning through practical activity

■ Some of the work needs to relate to the children's own culture and experience

■ The materials should include opportunities for pupil self-assessment

■ Designers must take account of reading age, and literacy levels within the family. Where necessary written materials need to be concise

■ There need to be strategies, including audio, for guiding and supporting children's reading

Quality, presentation and practical issues

■ The quality of the pack in terms of overall design and layout is a key factor. This includes quality of artwork and clarity of print

■ There must be clear instructions at every stage (with instructions clearly separated from learning text)

■ Artwork and pictures should be used to break up text

■ Some form of binding should be considered for workbooks (to prevent pages being lost or muddled)

■ The pack needs to contain all the materials a pupil will need, from basics such as pencils to reading/text books, videos and equipment for practical activities

■ Any equipment needs to be suitably robust

■ There needs to be a box file, or similar packaging, for the whole pack

These valuable pointers reflect ideas also developed by other TESs and shared with colleagues via conferences and unpublished reports. The emphasis is on careful pre-planning and is a reminder of the relatively constrained nature of the exchange of units of work once the travelling season gets underway. The problematic linkage illustrated by the dotting of the other side of the triangle.

The teacher, school and TES roles

Amundsen introduced her triangle as a way of focusing on the importance of taking a holistic approach to the design and delivery of distance learning. It is important to consider the actors and components, but equally important to consider the potential for interaction between them. As the EFECOT publication notes:

> All elements of the distance learning process, from the production of materials and use of work packs to management and support systems, need to be fully integrated and planned as a coherent whole. (*op cit*, 1994)

In the ideal good practice scenario the base school, supported by its TES, needs to sit at the centre of such an integrated approach. It needs to be aware of the cultural and practical dimensions of the challenge posed by its mobile pupils. And it needs to work to embrace parents as partners, and to play a central part in producing packs. The other part of the process, as seen from the perspective of the school, is perhaps best summed up in the word 'management'. How will the process be co-ordinated? How will pupils be prepared? How will the school try to maximise continuity? How will units of work be exchanged with families? How will progress be monitored? How will feedback be organised? How will communication and other forms of support be encouraged?

It is not surprising to find that these processes have worked best in schools with a commitment to inclusion and to their Traveller pupils. Another critical factor seems to have been the identification of a key member of staff who is prepared and able to coordinate effectively and to work closely with the local TES.

There are some useful specific recommendations in the literature. Pupils and parents should be given a thorough introduction to their packs before they travel. They should also be encouraged to discuss their travel patterns and to keep base schools informed. They should agree targets and processes for exchanging units of work. In the autumn, on their return to winter yards, they should come together to review progress.

Units should be designed and exchanged so that the pupil always has a realistic, but not overpowering, amount of work to do. Here one successful approach has been based on the three-unit block. The learner leaves with two units, returns the first when completed and works on the second. The third is sent as soon as the first is received at school. This process continues (with feedback) throughout the travelling season.

Experience also brings home the message that communication and support should not be seen as an afterthought. It needs to be planned in. Telephone contact should be encouraged, even structured in by, for example, having a member of staff available on the end of a phone for a fixed slot each week. Fax can also be useful; as explored by the Hampshire TES.

The Motifax project (Kenyon and Shannon, 2000) also highlighted some interesting ideas. This was an attempt to encourage student ownership by putting the pupil at the centre of a record-keeping process and including a simple reward system, a 'merit' card. From the base-school perspective it also drew attention to the importance of planning for supportive site visits by TES staff during the travelling period, as well as the supportive potential of any schools visited *en route.*

The potential role of ICT

The period 1996-2000 saw EFECOT coordinating a number of European projects to use ICT to enhance distance learning for Traveller pupils. The rationale for these projects was twofold. First, good interactive multimedia learning materials were already known to have an impact on pupil motivation and the emerging evidence suggested that they also had an impact on learning gains. Second, and more fundamental, new forms of mobile phone and satellite technology were increasingly allowing for wireless access to the Internet and to data transfer. Work could be varied, and messages exchanged, electronically. There was increasing potential to strengthen both the dotted sides of Amundsen's triangle and hence to reduce transactional distance.

These projects set out to use the leading edge technology of their time and have been written up elsewhere (Marks, 2003). Unfortunately, as is often the case with leading edge work, the main projects, TOPILOT, FLEX and Trapeze, did not bear immediate fruit. TOPILOT was successful in itself, but technology moved on before the system could be introduced in the UK. FLEX hit internal (technological) problems. Trapeze was a great success but involved what was, at that time, very expensive two-way satellite communication.

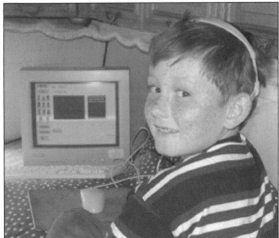

Children involved with the EFECOT projects.

However, the projects were important in two ways. They raised awareness about what could be achieved, and they involved a small number of TESs (Derby and Derbyshire, the Devon Consortium, Hertfordshire and the WMCESTC), with staff gaining direct experience of communication technologies and developing related ICT skills.

In a sense, what followed was a pregnant pause. Ironically, systematic Internet-based learning began to develop with other out-of-school children, in services with less experience of distance learning. Such initiatives included work with excluded pupils and with children who were sick and needed support at home. The difference was that these groupings of children could access the Internet from home through terrestrial telephone lines, or cable. Wireless technology remained less robust and more expensive.

A NATT survey conducted in 2003 showed that some TESs had begun to use laptops and CD ROM software with a small number of Traveller children, albeit frustrated by a lack of resources. It also identified a few initiatives which had been encouraging pupils to find ways of accessing the Internet whilst travelling and one project that tried to use wireless technology in a systematic way.

The wireless initiative, taken by the Hertfordshire Traveller Education Project working with the John Warner School, may well prove to be an important landmark. For the 2003 season, three pupils were provided with a laptop and a mobile phone to act as a modem to link them to the

Internet. Their History tasks were redesigned as interactive exercises. They were encouraged to access related websites. Some of their work was exchanged electronically with school and they were able to make use of email. As the report of this initiative makes clear, the impact on progress and motivation was significant and other subjects will now be added over time (Meadows and Stockdale, 2003).

Moving forward

The NATT coordinated a project funded by the Nuffield Foundation, which looked afresh at the potential of ICT to enhance distance learning for Traveller children (Marks, 2004). It was noted that by 2003 mobile telephony had become a more viable option and there are indications that one outcome of the Nuffield work will be a separate pilot project, supported by the DfES, which will use laptops, datacards[1] and GPRS data transfer systems[2] to strengthen links between primary base schools and mobile learners. The project also explored approaches to the challenge of secondary schooling.

Moving forward: a postscript

In adding this postscript it is pleasing to report that DfES backing and contributions from the Showmen's Guild of Great Britain, the National Association of Schoolmasters, Union of Women Teachers (NASUWT) and the mobile phone provider O2 made it possible to set up a new initiative called E-LAMP2. This new project has provided laptops and datacards for 20 primary age children during the 2004 travelling season. The children were supported by schools and TESs in four parts of the UK: Bolton, Cambridgeshire, South Gloucestershire and Surrey. A parallel initiative was also set up in Leicestershire. The approach has proved a resounding success in reducing transactional distance and the DfES has provided funding to consolidate this work and to extend it to four more TES regions for the 2005 travelling season. An interim report of this work has been published for the original Nuffield Foundation venture (Marks, 2004).

No doubt new lessons will continue to be learned as wireless communication hopefully becomes part of the design of frameworks for Traveller children, and new options like collaborative learning emerge. However, the various generalised 'traditional' ideas and insights drawn together in this chapter remain important for two reasons. The first is simply that change takes time. The second, and more fundamental, is that many of the lessons reflected in the documentation of the 1990s are timeless. They may need to be reinterpreted to take account of ICT enhancement, but the general principles about awareness, planning, design and management, and the stress on partnership between home, school and TES, will always be central.

Developments in ICT may also refocus questions about the balance of the relationship between base schools and TESs. This chapter reflects the documentation of the 1990s, written with the ideal of working towards a model with the base school at the helm and the TES in support.

In practice the balance seems to have been heavily dependent on particular and localised circumstances and on levels of resourcing. Success has been variable, and TESs have often had to take the major lead. This seems a particular challenge at the secondary level. Given school sizes, numbers of Traveller children are relatively small. Traveller commitment to secondary schooling is also more ambivalent, partly because of parental concerns about bullying and negative influences, but partly because community 'apprenticeship' views of education can come into conflict with 'schooling' priorities (Liégeois, 1998). Furthermore, the structure of secondary school is subject-specific and teachers have to handle work for large numbers of children across the year groupings. They are already faced with many and varied challenges, and, unlike their colleagues in primary schools, rarely have time to get to know individual pupils.

These factors indicate the challenge of effective KS3 and KS4 distance learning support for Traveller children and the importance of TES roles. If in future sensitive and appropriate work is to be designed and exchanged on a weekly basis – the norm in other distance learning services for children – and if pupils are to be encouraged to send emails and expect prompt responses, there are significant implications for staff skills and staff time. As the John Warner School initiative shows, success can be achieved when there are resources and commitment. And we have seen that new forms of specialised distance learning support are emerging for excluded pupils and those with medical needs, which are almost exclusively targeted at the secondary sector. This raises important questions about the entitlement of secondary-age mobile Traveller pupils to similar specialised provision – that is, specialised tutors and purpose-designed learning environments – and whether these may, in some contexts, offer a better alternative to the base school model. These possibilities are discussed in more detail in the final E-

LAMP report (Marks, 2004). New developments may well lead to new forms of TES/school partnership and future good practice may need to embrace new forms of institutional partnership in which new roles emerge.

Notes

1 A datacard is a card which contains an inbuilt aerial and can be slotted into a laptop. It can link a laptop to mobile telephone networks and gives access to the Internet, including access to email and to web-based resources.

2 GPRS is a system specially designed to transfer data across mobile telephone networks. It is potentially much faster than GSM (the normal system used for mobile telephone calls). It is also more robust in terms of handling weak signals and gaps in connectivity.

14

Still Travellers? – housed Travellers in a London borough

Jim Donovan

The concept of the housed Traveller can come as a surprise to teachers. Jim Donovan describes the variety of the housed Traveller client group in an urban setting, including Irish Travellers and East European Roma. He considers the difficulties schools face, including identifying the client group, and suggests how schools can involve, accommodate and reflect Travellers who are housed.

I write this chapter from the perspective of the *Gadze* – or *The Man* – who has appeared at the site gates and doorsteps of Irish Travellers, Eastern European Roma and some New Travellers in the inner London borough of Camden over the past seven years. The fact that most of the Travellers in Camden now live in houses has presented both the families and local services with challenges but we are coming to terms with them. They range from the mundane, as families cope with the management of a house, to the profound, as we weigh the psychological effects on Traveller children of growing up in the unnatural environment of a house, cut off from easy access to extended family and networks.

The background

Up to the late 1980s, Irish Travellers occupied verges, railway sidings, parks and roadsides across the London borough of Camden. The council's policy of limited toleration meant that families sometimes remained for weeks or even months on these illegal stopping places. By

1990 Camden Council had established three small tolerated sites – which later became permanent – whilst at the same time accelerating its evictions of unofficial encampments elsewhere in the borough. Doing this increased the number of families declaring themselves homeless and being moved into homeless families' accommodation. An unpublished report (London Boroughs Traveller Education Team, 1990) noted that the Travellers moved out of their caravans reluctantly and were soon experiencing isolation and discrimination in their housing accommodation.

At the time I was co-ordinator of a community centre in Kilburn, an area of north London with a large Irish population. Traveller children came in just to have a look around the centre occasionally. They asked for nothing and talked a lot. They were full of life and interested in everything. Some years later, when I was an Education Social Worker for Travellers, I visited these same children, who were now teenagers, living in council flats. They were very different now – often stressed and unhappy. We need to try and understand the stresses housed Travellers have to cope with.

The client group – Irish Travellers/East European Roma

Initially the Traveller Education Service (TES) worked with Irish Travellers on unauthorised encampments and had some success placing children in local primary schools which had vacancies. As families moved from caravans into homeless families' accommodation and then to permanent housing, the TES came to recognise that mobility was not the only educational issue. There were challenges concerning Travellers' access to education long after they had moved into permanent accommodation.

Roma started to arrive in Camden seeking asylum from Eastern Europe in 1993, and joined the Irish Travellers as major clients of the TES in Camden and other London boroughs. Irish Travellers' strong cultural identity is derived from a nomadic way of life that few contemporary Eastern European Roma have experienced, so when the *Traveller Education Service* approached the Roma they were sometimes bemused, sometimes amused. Here were Travellers who had been housed for generations and who no longer had a relationship with the road, but whose lifestyle and attitudes showed many similarities to the geographically and historically separate Irish Travellers. Ironically, these Roma asylum seekers are often rendered highly mobile by the instability of their housing. The effect of being in housing for these Roma may not in itself be an educational issue but, housed or not, they continue to demonstrate the resilience and strength of nomadic heritages, and this manifests itself in their often strained relationship with an education system that tries to assimilate their children.

Camden TES – characteristics of good practice

The Camden TES provides support to Traveller families, at home and in school. The service operates on the principle that Traveller children should get the best possible education on offer, normally within a mainstream setting, and that TES support is additional to all the other professional input every child is entitled to. The TES has developed certain good practices in response to the needs of housed Travellers and Roma. They include:

- a flexible and pro-active approach that can respond to changing needs and enable a human response to problems

- use of frequent face to face contact as the primary form of communication

- monitoring educational access and achievement

- carefully targeted teaching interventions as part of a written support agreement with school

- rapid interventions with children who are out of school or absent

- practical assistance where this supports school attendance and achievement.

I have found good TES practice to be characterised by a set of flexible and purposeful attitudes and approaches rather than a rigid code. Good practice is good practice because it is inclusive and works for everyone.

Identifying the client group

Camden TES serves a scattered Traveller community, with no focal sites and with most families isolated in public housing. Consequently, identifying where Travellers are in the borough, and establishing what the issues are for each family, have become central to the work of the TES.

Most housed Travellers do not identify themselves to authorities and, while respecting this wish, we must also try to deliver a specialist service. Some families have been known to the TES for generations, on sites and in houses, and we have been able to maintain contact through the generations, which is often how we meet new families. Otherwise we monitor lists of homeless families, school admissions, exclusions, education welfare referrals and special educational needs panel minutes and rely on referrals from colleagues in housing, social services, schools and other TESs.

Families have been happy to accept TES support when introduced by a relative or friend. However, others make it clear they do not want to be associated with the TES and may say they are 'no longer Travellers' in which case we respect their privacy and leave them with TES contact details. In each circumstance we have to use judgement to decide whether we can be of help to housed Travellers in a way that is not intrusive.

Identifying the client group – TES links

Formal and informal networks between TESs for transferring and sharing knowledge about and responsibility for Traveller children provides a model for good practice as the client group moves between authorities. This has taken on a new relevance with the introduction of Identification, Referral and Tracking (IRT) systems for all children at risk from social exclusion (DfES Children and Young People's Unit, 2003), prompted by the recommendations of the Victoria Climbié Inquiry (2003). By contact between TESs, one housed Traveller family who moved between four LEAs in under a year was tracked and offered support each time they arrived at a new address. Another family who had four addresses and six schools within Camden had uninterrupted support from the TES.

Identifying the client group – PLASC data

In September 2002, LEAs collected PLASC (Pupil Level Annual School Census) data using the revised ethnic categories, which now include recognition of specific Traveller groups, namely, Travellers of Irish Heritage (WIRT) and Gypsy/Roma Travellers (WROM). This survey has thrown new light on the number of Travellers who, protectively, resist identifying their children as Travellers or Roma. Some of the most confident housed Traveller and Roma parents I have met did not identify their children to schools thus, as they believed it would cause them to be stereotyped, and also that teachers would immediately form low expectations of them.

The present figures show that in most areas the majority of Travellers known to local TESs describe themselves under non Traveller categories. In Camden, just 25 per cent of Travellers and Roma identified themselves as such. The figures do not distinguish between Travellers in caravans and those who are housed but it is expected that housed Travellers are least likely to identify themselves to schools. This has coincided with a growing awareness that there are Travellers in housing and how severely their needs may be ignored. Emerging awareness of the needs of housed Travellers recently led to the abandonment of the two year rule[1] whereby families who had been settled for two years were considered to no longer require specialist support from a TES. Unfortunately, planning authorities still take the view that being a Traveller is a lifestyle choice rather than a cultural identity – as is illustrated when Travellers who have moved temporarily into housing cease to be recognised as Travellers for the purposes of planning applications.

A housed Traveller grandmother approaching a local secondary school for places told me:

> Because they know they're Traveller girls they just don't want them, they give the places to other people.

Being housed – being invisible?
Housed Travellers have the option to conceal their ethnicity in a way that Travellers seen to live in caravans can not. The experience of generations of racism has led many Travellers to conceal their identity. Ian Hancock writes in his article *The Struggle for the Control of Identity* (1997) 'I know of very few Roma who weren't warned as children to keep their ethnicity to themselves.'

Travellers cultivate their invisibility as a protection against harassment but also because they are seldom offered support similar to that currently afforded most other ethnic minorities. Such enforced invisibility can undermine the children's need to have a cultural identity they can freely express and enjoy. It may put the children into a confusing and stressful position, particularly in the close atmosphere of a school. In the years I have been dealing with poor school attendance issues, a recurring theme has been the expression by housed Irish Traveller children that they feel different from their peers and that they don't belong in a classroom situation. For no apparent reason, they feel people are looking at them, talking about them and thinking critical thoughts about them. As one 14 year-old housed Traveller girl refusing to attend school put it: 'I felt like they were teasing me, although they never said anything'.

Being housed – being different

The academically competitive environment of a classroom doubtless heightens the anxiety of children who join a class at an educational disadvantage and some Traveller children in Camden self-exclude. One boy said the reason for his poor behaviour was that he felt like an 'alien'. This has led to exclusions from school. For housed Irish Travellers 'feeling different' is a feeling that has no obvious explanation – they are white, English speaking Christian families living in houses. Travellers in caravans have a visibly different lifestyle whereas housed Traveller children may be asked to explain behaviours and feelings that they themselves do not fully understand.

Many Traveller children grow up with the confident belief that they were born with an education and learn all they need to know from family role models and by taking part in all aspects of the domestic and economic life of the family. Schooling is seen as there merely to supplement self-education by providing literacy and numeracy skills. Housed Traveller children may be denied access to the unique Traveller curriculum and, perhaps more significantly, to its affirmation of Traveller ideals, self-belief and identity.

The relationship between majority society and Travellers, particularly those in housing, has been brought into greater focus in recent years with the debates, experiments and legislation that seek to modify the behaviours of not just children but whole families. Anti-Social Behaviour Orders, Parenting Orders, increased penalties for truancy and more stringent housing policies are designed to promote models of behaviour against which a Traveller way of life is made to appear as deviant.

Occasionally, local residents have taken matters into their own hands by collecting petitions to have Traveller families evicted. Housed Travellers, often accommodated in the pressurised atmosphere of highly populated run-down housing estates, may be seen to overstep the 'normal' boundaries of housed living in ways that attract negative attention. This criticism can gather its own momentum, particularly when stimulated by anti-Traveller racism. For example, the family may live more of their lives outside the flat or house than is considered normal. Their lives can be observed by their neighbours: the young children, to whom families give more independence, are much in evidence, and the many comings and goings of numerous extended family members and friends are much in evidence. Consequently housed Traveller families are more likely to have interventions from the authorities, who will seek to apply inappropriate standards when making judgements about their lifestyle.

I recently visited a family of ten, rehoused after an eviction, who said they were being routinely associated with every incident of vandalism, noise and violence that happened in the street. Neighbours have been quick to contact Social Services and the Housing authorities. The family was moved into the most run-down property in the street, with little furniture and equipment, and soon attracted negative attention as they struggled to cope. They felt under attack and their concern about the children's safety had been heightened, with implications for their attending school.

'It's not natural to keep the children locked up all day, but people are watching them all the time', observed an Irish Traveller father newly moved into a terraced house.

House v. trailer, house v. site

The family's routines may have developed in a caravan so that adult and child routines have to be managed to coincide in a single space – something their settled neighbours see as inappropriate. The informal childcare sharing possible between extended family members on a site is unavailable in the sprawling dead ends and stairwells of a housing estate. Conducting aspects of your life outside is essential when living in a caravan, but what a Traveller family may see as the healthy enactment of their lively extended family life can be interpreted by neighbours as the signs of a dissolute and dysfunctional lifestyle.

Being housed – the challenges

Settled life in a house exposes families to more written correspondence and this can cause difficulties when literacy is low. TESs have an important role in helping parents understand and deal with letters from schools and in encouraging schools to communicate verbally. Misunderstood or unintelligible correspondence leading to missed appointments and deadlines has, in my experience, led to serious problems with secondary transfers, special needs assessments and much else.

Travellers who are moved from caravans into housing face a battery of challenges that are practical, organisational, social and economic. They may have little furniture or domestic equipment they can bring in, but buying this all in one go is a huge expense few can afford. Replicating the tidy and well-ordered interior of a caravan in a poorly maintained and ill-equipped house may be impossible. For a young mother who has grown up doing household chores in the company of sisters and cousins, living alone is a new experience that has to be met without support on hand. Parents' informal control is weakened when their children widen their social circle to include non Traveller children whose families are unaccountable, unlike their neighbours on a site. A housed Traveller mother of child excluded from school said of her daughter 'She acts likes she's grown up, but she's only 11 and big kids on this estate take advantage and lead her into trouble'.

For centuries, Travellers have relied on the family to provide virtually everything to sustain them in a society from which they felt excluded. The family became the primary source of care, education, social inter-action and prosperity. Housed families are isolated from relatives and traditional support networks. That may be why some families fail to settle in their house and always seem prepared to move on. I know a family who drive their primary age children to a school fifty minutes away every day, as this school has established a relationship with the local site where most of this family's relatives live.

A young Traveller mother of four who recently moved into housing for the first time told us that she had no experience of running a house, which requires decorating, furnishing and so on. So it was a struggle to organise the home and pay for furniture. The family was uncomfort-able about sleeping on separate levels and the children were showing signs of anxiety. Like many Traveller families, when she moved out of her caravan she had no furniture and few possessions. Her concern that people would see such problems as evidence of neglectful parenting was heightened when a neighbour contacted Social Services on grounds that the children were 'out of control'.

An Irish Traveller mother who had moved to a housing estate told me 'I don't like living in a flat but I want the children to have a chance to get an education.'

Not only was she trying to settle in an unfamiliar environment but she also felt a strong psychological pull to rejoin her close relations on sites outside London. When they were with these relatives, her children felt a sense of belonging and wanted to stay and not return to their flat and school. The mother had the difficult task of negotiating between family loyalty and her children attending school. The school was alarmed at the number of days missed and refused to authorise absences, so I appealed for some flexibility, saying in a report: 'Mother felt compelled to go (to visit her sick uncle) as it is expected among Traveller families that the family should gather at times of severe illness. She stayed there as long as she felt she had to.' Local schools with experience of Irish Travellers and Roma are coming to accept the particular cultural imperatives that apply to these communities, whether housed or not.

Schools that listen

The obligations arising from close attachment to a scattered extended family often affect school attendance. Commitment to the family requires Traveller children to be actively involved in religious events, family crises and celebrations, and their failure to do so can lead to bad feeling in the family. For housed Travellers, who do not have easy daily access to family, these events are highly significant in maintaining essential bonds with a family network that may extend far and wide. Family bonding is also strengthened by the children staying with relatives for spells during the year, sometimes in an attempt to keep them in touch with life on a site. Indeed the extended Traveller family has a fundamental and positive role that is applauded by governments and often sought by settled people.

My advice to schools is to encourage families to be open about their future plans, not feel they have to be secretive. This makes it possible to negotiate and plan in the best interests of the children's education and ensure maximum attendance. Schools need to acknowledge the importance to Travellers of family events and religious ceremonies and be willing to compromise, and it may require extra understanding in the case of housed Travellers.

Welcoming schools

Every family will appreciate a truly inclusive school, one that is welcoming, communicative and friendly, regardless of the family's circumstances, time of arrival or the interrupted learning of the children. And it is vital for newly arrived housed Travellers, who may not have the support of a TES. While integrating a newly arrived child into secondary school after two years out of school, what was most effective was establishing one friendly face among the staff to whom the child and parents could turn.

In a mainstream educational climate dominated by targets and results, the outcomes of TES good practice with housed Travellers can appear modest or even insignificant. Children who arrive with educational disadvantage must have their progress highlighted and celebrated promptly if they are to be encouraged to go further. A deficit approach to Traveller performance which focuses on what they can't do rather than what they can do is to be avoided.

> The kids were bullied at first because they are travelling children, but the school quickly talked to the other children and sorted it and now we are very happy with that school. *Housed Irish Traveller woman taking care of two of her grandchildren*

Traveller/school interface
Workers in Traveller Education are at the borders between society at large and Travellers. They apply pressure on Travellers to conform. So that compromise is on both sides, TESs must intervene in schools to promote respect for the unique lifestyles arising out of nomadic heritages, while they negotiate increased educational access for the children. That this is a process developing over generations, not weeks, must continually be communicated to schools and LEAs. I recently persuaded a family to postpone their annual journey to visit relatives outside London, as their daughter's school attendance was already critically low – another example of persuading Traveller cultures to accommodate the majority society's standards and principles. The effect of this may be greater on housed Travellers who cannot employ the traditional defence mechanism of mobility and avoidance.

The increasing availability and distribution of learning resources that celebrate nomadic heritages in the broad sense are now appearing in circle times and on classroom displays. Schools need to explore ways to nurture Traveller and Roma culture wherever possible, and to help the children of housed Travellers retain the independent spirit that has characterised Travellers for generations.

In one Camden secondary school, fourteen Roma students have become happy to be recognised as Roma (and not Polish nor Czech) by *gadje* in school. When they made a video, *Introduction to our School*, in Romany and it was watched by the headteacher and parents, their nervousness and pride were clear to see.

In another school, a small group of Irish Traveller boys at risk of exclusion have been helped to use art in weekly sessions to enable quiet reflection and to offer some insight into their distracted and angry behaviour. This school has also begun to enrol Traveller boys onto one of the emerging school-based vocational programmes that may meet the boys' desire to learn practical skills that could enable a future self-employed occupation. The introduction of flexible learning models in the new Entry to Employment (E2E) programme similarly suggests that the education of Traveller teenagers is becoming more promising and relevant.

Conclusion

Travellers have struggled for centuries to maintain their way of life and principles and some now do so in houses. While Travellers on the road have always had to fight to maintain their travelling way of life, those now in houses suffer a second turn of the screw, by having their identity threatened and denied. Travellers and non Travellers working in education must continue to find safe ways for housed Traveller children to recognise, learn about, take part in and express their heritage and schools should continue to promote awareness of housed Travellers within the education system.

Note

1 Previous legislation governing the funding of TESs stipulated that those supported should not have been housed for more than two years. This stipulation does not apply to the Standards Fund, Vulnerable Children's Fund grant (Ed).

Appendix 1

An example of whole school curriculum plan to address the needs of Traveller pupils. Context, a secondary school near a Fairground wintering yard. Twelve Traveller pupils on roll, all of whom experience interrupted education during the school year.

Objectives	Strategies/Processes	Key Success Criteria (including quantitative targets where appropriate)	Monitoring/Evaluation processes	6. Lead responsibilities
To raise the achievement of Traveller pupils in school through the development and implementation of support structures in the school.	• Ensure base line assessment is completed for all Travellers	• To raise National Curriculum levels by at least one third	• Data base	• Subject teachers, LSU and Traveller Education Project (TEP)
	• Identify Specific learning difficulties (SpLD) and other SEN needs and implement a suitable support programme	• All pupils to have completed baseline testing	• Learning Support Unit (LSU) records	• Senco
		• In class support in place.	• Written records	• LSA and subject teachers
	• A reading recovery programme, Additional Literacy Support, or 1:1 support will be set up where specific needs are identified	• Reading Recovery Programme and Additional Literacy Support in place	• LSU records	• Senco
	• Create IEP's where necessary	• IEP's in place		
	• Apply for additional funding where appropriate	• Traveller culture reflected in the curriculum at least once in the school year and highlighted in departmental plans	• LSU to regularly check	• Senco
	• Seek opportunities to reflect Traveller culture in the curriculum where appropriate	• At least six books in the library reflecting Traveller culture	• Liaison with Heads of Department (HODs)	• TEP and HOD
			• Meeting with librarian on a regular basis	• TEP, librarian and LSU

Objectives	Strategies/Processes	Key Success Criteria (including quantitative targets where appropriate)	Monitoring/Evaluation processes	6. Lead responsibilities
To raise staff awareness of cultural issues and seek opportunities to reflect Traveller culture in the curriculum	• Involve TEP in Inset • Liaison between LSU and staff • Pupils given the opportunity to talk to form tutors about their lifestyle. (PSE)	• At least one Inset delivered to whole school per academic year • Termly contact through SEN link group • Termly meeting of pupil and form tutor	• Feedback from staff • Minutes of meetings • Report from tutor/PSE co-ordinator	• TEP • Senco • Form tutor PSE co-ordinator
To enhance home school liaison	• LSU and TEP to be present and be introduced at new year intake sessions • Encourage pupils and parents to inform school of predicted mobility • Ensure pupils and parents meet with Senco or EWO before travelling • Regular communication with pupils and parents whilst on site • Communicate regularly with pupils whilst off site	• SENCO and TEP meet with all parents and pupils at new intake evening • Log of mobility in place • Log set up and contact made at least once per half term • Contact made at least twice a month • Dates forwarded to pupils	• Log of meetings • Log up to date • Log up to date • Log up to date • Dates received	

To enhance home school liaison. (continued)	• Communicate regularly with pupils whilst off site	• Pupils can scan and send e-mails	• Log of messages received
	• Inform pupils who are off site of important dates in their school calendar that will help them feel included in school life	• 90% attendance whilst on site	• Check database
		• 50% of parents to attend one consultation evening per academic year	• Log of attendance of parents
	• Ensure pupils have basic IT skills to use scanner, e-mail		
	• Attendance to be monitored by EWO and concerns discussed with senior staff and Traveller education welfare officer	• Log of all e-mail and mobile phone numbers available in contact book	• Data base set up
	• Encourage parents to attend consultation meetings whenever possible	• Newsletter sent out regularly	• Newsletter received
	• Obtain mobile telephone numbers and e-mail addresses		
	• Send out school newsletters regularly to pupils off site		

Appendix 2

Example of handout from *Literacy for All* participant pack
Literacy for All guidance for planning a unit of work to
support Black, bilingual and Traveller pupils

- Select an appropriate text which lends itself to the promotion of inclusion and cultural diversity. A text can be fiction, non-fiction, poetry or not even a book e.g. a poster

- Identify on your medium-term plan, which objectives would best support this task. Ensure you have 1 or 2 reading objectives, and 1 or 2 linked writing objectives. Ensure that appropriate sentence and word level objectives are identified

- Plan for a unit of work over 1 or 2 weeks

- Plan shared reading activities which lead into shared writing. Children's reading will then provide the model for their writing. The plan should have at least a 50 / 50 balance of time spent teaching each. With older children, weight the plan towards time spent teaching writing. Ensure the activities you plan provide children with a clear audience and purpose for their writing

- Within the shared session, be explicit about what you are teaching, not just the activity you are doing

- Write in the word or sentence level activity you are doing. Show how you are linking sentence level teaching to text level teaching in shared writing. Include some of the ideas from the Grammar for Writing book

- Map across the week which group you will be working with in guided work, and whether it is reading or writing. If children have targets, you could show which target is the focus for that week's guided session, and how you will be supporting children in achieving their targets. Ensure the teacher supports each group once

■ Plan in support and input from Cambridgeshire Race Equality and Diversity Service staff, and show how you are working together e.g. by sharing the teaching of the shared session, doing a joint role play/interview/hot-seating

■ Plan in support of Teaching Assistants and Bilingual Assistants, showing which groups they will be working with

■ Plan in phonic games, or whole class interactive spelling games at KS2

■ Plan for independent activities which have a strong link with the shared session, and give children an opportunity to apply and consolidate what you have taught them. If appropriate, plan for one piece of writing over a number of days, showing each stage of the writing process – planning, drafting, editing, improving, presenting

■ Include opportunities for ICT e.g. in shared or guided work, as independent activities using software or word processing

■ The plan should provide opportunities for use of first language where possible, speaking and listening activities, visual outcomes e.g. a story map, literacy based play where appropriate, story boxes, role play, the listening centre, reading games

■ Plan for the use of the plenary for assessment and for consolidating the learning objective. Identify an independent group on the plan to 'home in' on for checking understanding

■ In your planning you might like to refer to the National Literacy Strategy Guidance, Supporting Pupils with English as an Additional Language

Appendix 3

Example page from Monitoring and Evaluating Inclusive Practice for Gypsy and Traveller Pupils: A Self-Review for Schools

Ofsted Framework 2003 **Ofsted Evaluation Schedule Standards achieved by pupils** **Key Question 3.1 – How high are standards achieved in the areas of learning, subjects and courses of the curriculum?** 1 Inspectors must interpret and report on the school's analysis of how different groups of pupils perform. 2 The main judgments concern whether the achievements of the pupils are as high as they should be, taking account of their capabilities and the progress they have made in the school.	
Questions regarding Gypsy and Traveller pupils	**School Self evaluation**
Does the school monitor and analyse the attainment of Gypsy and Traveller pupils at each stage?	
Does the school analyse the progress made from one stage to the next?	
Are there any variations in achievement between the different subjects?	
How do the Gypsy and Traveller children compare to other groups?	
What use does the school make of this information?	
Can the school identify those Gypsies and Travellers who are underachieving?	
Do they know the reason for this (intermittent schooling, culture, learning difficulties)?	
How well do you support Gypsies and Travellers to achieve as much as they can by overcoming barriers to learning?	
Do you know the trends in the school's results with Gypsy and Traveller pupils over time?	
Do you know the achievements of Gypsy and Traveller children in other local schools?	

References and further reading

Amundsen, C (1993) The Evolution of Theory in Distance Education, in Keegan D. (ed) *Theoretical Principles of Distance Education*, London: Routledge

Bhopal, K, Gundar, J, James, C and Owen, C (2000) *Working Towards Inclusive Education: Aspects of Good*

Practice for Gypsy Traveller Pupils, Nottingham: DfEE Research Report RR238

Black, P. and William, D. (1998) *Inside the black box: raising standards through classroom assessment*

Buckinghamshire County Council (2002) *Guidance for schools dealing with racist incidents*

Conteh, Jean (2003) *Succeeding in diversity culture, language and learning in primary classrooms*, Stoke on Trent: Trentham

DES (1985) *Education for All, the Report of the Committee of Enquiry into the Education of Children from Ethnic Minority Groups* (The Swann Report), London: HMSO

Devon Traveller Education Service (1998) *Get it Sorted*, Totnes, DTES

Devon Consortium Traveller Education Service (1999) *Fair Comment: Parents' views of Distance Learning*, Totnes, DCTES

DfEE (1997) *Letter to Headteachers*

DfES (1998) *Are we missing out?* Video. London: DfES

DfES (1999) *Supporting Pupils Learning English as an Additional Language*, National Literacy Strategy

DfES (2001) *Special Educational Needs Code of Practice*, DfES/581/2001

DfES (2001a) *Supporting the Target Setting Process*, DfES/0065/2001

DfES (2003) *Aiming High: Raising the Achievement of Gypsy Traveller Pupils, a Guide to Good Practice*, Nottingham: DfES/0443/2003

DfES (2003a) *Excellence and enjoyment: a strategy for Primary schools*, Nottingham: DfES

DfES Children and Young People's Unit (2003b) *Referral and tracking systems*

DfES/National Association of Teachers of Travellers (2002) *Record of Educational Development* (RED) book – contains information for parents and schools on educational assessments and records of accumulative targets, DfES/NATT

EFECOT (1994) *What is your School doing for Travelling Children: a guide to equal opportunities through distance learning*, Brussels, EFECOT

Essex County Council (2001) *A World of Opportunities: a working guide to equal opportunities practice*, Essex County Council

Hancock, I (1997) The Struggle for the Control of Identity in *Transitions* Vol. 4

Holmes, P, Knaepkens, L, and Marks, K (2001) Fighting Social Exclusion through ODL: the development of initiatives with the children of Traveller communities, in Trindade, A.R. (ed) *New Learning*, Lisbon, Universidade Aberta

Jordan, E (1996) Education for Travellers, in Befring, E (ed) *Teacher Education for Equality,* Association for Teacher Education in Europe

Kenrick, K and Clarke, C (1999) *Moving On: The Gypsies and Travellers of Britain,* Hatfield, University of Hertfordshire Press.

Kiddle, C (1999) *Traveller Children. A Voice for Themselves,* Jessica Kingsley

Kindersley, B and Kindersley, A (1999) *Children of Britain Just Like Me,* London: Dorling

Liégeois, JP (1998) *School Provisions for Ethnic Minorities: The Gypsy Paradigm,* Hatfield, University of Hertfordshire Press

Lloyd, G *et al* (1999) Teachers and Gypsy Travellers, *Scottish Educational Review,* 31 (1)

Macpherson, W *et al* (1999) *The Stephen Lawrence Inquiry Report,* London: Stationery Office,

Marks, K (2003) EFECOT: Supporting the Travelling Tradition, in Bradley J.(ed) *The Open Classroom: distance learning in and out of schools,* London, Kogan Page

Marks, K (2004) *Traveller Education – changing times, changing technologies,* Stoke on Trent: Trentham

Meadows, P and Stockdale, K (2003) *To raise the achievement of Traveller pupils at The John Warner School through using ICT in Distance Learning.* Hatfield, Hertfordshire Traveller Education Project and The John Warner School.

Moore, M.G. (1991) Editorial: Distance Education Theory, *The American Journal of Distance Education,* Vol. 5 No. 3: pps 1-6

Ofsted (1996) *The education of Travelling children – A report from the Office of Her Majesty's Chief Inspector of Schools,* London: Ofsted Ref. HMR/12/96/NS

Ofsted (1999) *Raising the attainment of minority ethnic pupils – school and LEA responses,* London: Ofsted Refd. HMI 170

Ofsted (2001a) *The National Literacy Strategy: The third year,* London: Ofsted Ref. HMI 332

Ofsted (2001b) *Managing support for the attainment of pupils from minority ethnic groups,* London: Ofsted Ref. 157

Ofsted (2002a) *Evaluating educational inclusion – guidance for inspectors and schools,* London: Ofsted Ref. HMI 235

Ofsted (2002b) *The National Literacy Strategy: the first four years 1998-2002,* London: Ofsted Ref. HMI 555

Ofsted (2003) *Inspecting schools: framework for inspecting schools,* London: Ofsted

Ofsted/Audit Commission inspection guidance (2002) *Required inspection judgement 16 support to schools in raising standards of minority ethnic and Traveller children,* London: Ofsted

Rowntree D. (1992) *Exploring Open and Distance,* Learning London, Kogan Page

Save the Children (2000) *Denied a future? The right to education of Roma/Gypsy and Traveller Children in Europe,* SCUK

Save the Children (2001) *In Safe Hands,* SCUK

Sylva, K, Siraj-Blatchford, I and Taggart, B (2003) *Assessing quality in the early years.* Stoke on Trent: Trentham

Telford and Wrekins' Children's Fund, West Midlands Consortium Education Service for Travelling Children, *Move On, Move Up* video, Wolverhampton: WMCESTC

Wragg, T (1999) Keynote address at the Edinburgh/TESS conference, Edinburgh

Resources for children

Cambridgeshire Multicultural Education Service (2002) *Moving On* (CD and Lesson plans), Cambridge: Cambridgeshire County Council

Cambridgeshire Multicultural Education Service (2002) *Plaits and Braids* (poster and lesson plans), Cambridge: Cambridgeshire County Council

Cunningham, Kathleen (1997) *A Moving Way of Life*, Cambridge: Cambridgeshire County Council

Delamere A. and Norton P. (2002) *The Travelling People KS2 Activity Pack*

Doherty, Berlie (1992) *Snowy*, London: Picture Lions

Essex County Council (1995) *Traveller Alphabet*, Essex County Council

Hertfordshire Traveller Education Project (1999) *Monday Morning*, Hertford: Herts. TEP

Hiçyilmaz, Gaye (2000) *Girl in Red*, London: Dolphin Paperbacks

Hird, Margaret and Whitwell, Ann (1999) *A Horse for Joe*, Trowbridge: Wiltshire Traveller Education

info@artefactstoorder.com *A Suitcase of History* info@artefactstoorder.com

Kindersley, Barnabas and Anabel (1999) *Children of Britain Just Like Me*, London: Dorling Kindersley

Madden, Sandy (1999) *Melissa to the Rescue*, Great Britain: Avon Consortium Traveller Education Service

Norfolk County Council (1994) *Silly Jake.* Norwich: Norfolk CC

Norfolk County Council (1994) *A close knit community* Video, Norwich: Norfolk CC

Norfolk County Council (1994) *Counting Book 1*, Norwich: Norfolk CC

Norfolk County Council (1994) *Counting Book 2*, Norwich: Norfolk CC

Norfolk County Council (1994) *Travellers at fairs and festivals – A talkabout book, book 1*, Norwich: Norfolk CC

Norfolk County Council (1994*) Families at Appleby Horse Fair, a talkabout book, Book 2*, Norwich: Norfolk CC

Norfolk County Council (1994) *Amber and Anne, a talkabout book, book 3*, Norwich: Norfolk CC

Norfolk Traveller Education Service (1995) *Sean's Wellies*, Norwich: Norfolk TES

Norfolk Traveller Education Service (2001) *Ruby's rabbits*, Norwich: Norfolk TES

Parker, Lena (1999) *My Gran*, Cambridge: Cambridgeshire Team for Traveller Education

Smith E D M (2002) *The Smiths*, National Association of Teachers of Travellers

Taylor, Karen (1999) *The Broken Broomstick,* Cheshire Traveller Education Service

West Midlands Consortium Education Service for Travelling Children *Literacy trail,* Wolverhampton: WMCESTC

Williams, Beryl (1999) *Stone Soup,* Oxfordshire: The Advisory Service for the Education of Travellers

Williamson, Duncan (1993) *Fireside Tales of the Traveller Children,* Edinburgh: Canongate Silkies

Wormington, A. *et al* (2000) *The Travelling People* and Wormington A. *et al* (2000) *The Travelling People Big Book,* London: Hackney, Newham and Tower Hamlets Traveller Education Services (See also Delamere, A. and Norton, P.)

Wright, Kit (1987) *Cat Among the Pigeons,* Viking Kestrel

About the authors

Lucy Beckett is Head of the Oxfordshire Advisory Service for the Education of Travellers and is currently President of the National Association of Teachers of Travellers.

Barbara Blaney has been a teacher for thirty years and involved in Traveller Education for the last eighteen. Currently Head of Learning Support at Chalvedon Comprehensive School in Basildon, Essex, Barbara has been privileged to be invited to attend Traveller christenings, weddings and funerals.

Lorna Daymond taught in several primary schools in Kent and Norfolk before becoming Head of the Norfolk Traveller Education Service in 1986. Her other roles have included ten years as a manufacturing jeweller, owning and running a rural art gallery, and writing plays for BBC Radio. She is married with three grown-up children.

Jim Donovan is an Inclusion Officer for Travellers, he has spent virtually his whole career working in Camden. After 19 years as youth and community worker, city farm manager and community centre co-ordinator, he took a Social Work degree before joining Camden LEA as Education Social Worker, becoming ESW for Travellers in 1996.

Brian Foster coordinates and monitors the work of seven London Traveller Education Services. He has worked as a teacher and local government officer, promoting the inclusion and opportunities of Gypsy Travellers in the UK. He has organised courses and worked as a consultant in Europe, and is on the management committee of the Irish Travellers movement.

Sue Green is an Advisory and Support Teacher on the secondary team of the Durham and Darlington Education Service for Travelling Children. She has worked across all age ranges from nursery to further education. She has a particular interest in curriculum development and is currently developing an independent learning pack on the theme of Citizenship. As a volunteer youth worker, she trains young people in outdoor activities.

Hilary Horton became aware of issues confronting Gypsy Travellers while working at ILEA's Centre for Urban Educational Studies, then joined the Inner London Education Authority Teachers for Travellers team. She became Advisory Teacher for Travellers and Literacy in Camden and is now Literacy Consultant in the Camden Primary Strategy Team.

Sue Itzinger taught for six years in a secondary modern in Pontefract. She joined Leeds Traveller Service in 1988 and has been involved with transition, 14-16 Curriculum and training. She is interested in all aspects of special needs, especially Dyslexia.

Arthur Ivatts OBE trained as a teacher and youth leader. He worked full-time for ACERT (Advisory Committee for the Education of Romany and other Travellers) and was recruited as Her Majesty's Inspector of schools and soon given national responsibility for the education of Travellers. He works now as an international specialist consultant on Gypsy and Roma issues in the UK and Europe.

Anne Jefford is a support teacher who has worked for the Traveller Education Project in Hertfordshire for 20 years, developing responses to distance learning and improving responses to secondary attendance and achievement. She works full time in the classroom, collaborating with mainstream staff to ensure Traveller pupils are being fully accessed to the curriculum.

Ken Marks is a Research Associate in the Inclusive Education and Equality Research Centre, at the Department of Educational Studies. In his eight years at the Centre his work has had a European focus, supporting initiatives supported by EFECOT. He is interested in using new technologies to support Traveller children and has produced a report on the E-Learning and Mobility project (E-LAMP) for the Nuffield Foundation: *Traveller Education – changing times, changing technologies.*

METAS, the Traveller Team from the Minority Ethnic and Traveller Achievement Service supports Traveller families in Buckinghamshire. The Team promotes access, attendance, achievement and continuity by empowering parents, educationalists and other agencies through home-school-community links, developing resources and removing the barriers to learning. Linda Lewins and teacher Malcolm Wilson wrote the chapter. Kit Couper, Maureen Starkey and everyone in the team supported the Traveller children and schools mentioned.

Claire Norris is Assistant Manager of Education Leeds Travellers Education Service. She worked in primary schools in Newham and Leeds before joining the TES in 1983. She has worked with all the Travelling communities, teaching on sites, in mobile classrooms and in educational establishments.

Kate Stockdale taught in primary schools before starting with the Hertfordshire Traveller Education Project in 1990. She has a particular interest in using ICT to enhance distance learning and was involved in an EFECOT project to use two way satellite communications. She is currently working with secondary school colleagues to develop electronic learning materials to support distance learning and piloting the use of laptops and WAP phones.

Lousie Stokoe worked as a Welfare Officer and for the past three years has been a Specialist Education Officer for the Durham and Darlington Education Service for Travelling Children with Gypsy and Traveller young people aged 0-25 years.

Chris Tyler has worked in the field of Traveller education throughout the UK and Europe. Trained as an English teacher, he worked in secondary schools and an off site unit in London before joining Roberts Brothers Super Circus as their travelling teacher in 1988. After co-ordinating the European Federation for the Education of the Children of Occupational Travellers' circus working group across Europe, he joined the London Borough of Hillingdon, leading their peripatetic Traveller Education Support Service. He became head of the Hertfordshire Traveller Education Project in 1997. He has also written *The Wall at the End of the Site*, a children's fiction book.

Carol Ward taught for ten years in a special school and is in her sixteenth year with Leeds Travellers Education Service, developing their work in exciting ways. She is involved in training and new initiatives for improving attendance, such as a booklet of successful Travellers.

Kanta Wild-Smith is Area Manager (South) for the Essex and Southend Consortium Traveller Education Service, an advisory support teacher and manager of the Family Learning Development Project within the Service. She was President of the National Association of Teachers of Travellers 1997-2000 and worked with DfES on *Aiming High, Raising the Achievement of Gypsy/Traveller Pupils, Good Practice Guide for Schools*.

Margaret Wood has been interested in Traveller Education since working at the Gypsy Summer School in Wisbech in the early '70s. She taught languages in secondary schools and is now Team Manager for Traveller Education with Cambridgeshire Race Equality and Diversity Service.

Index